Comments from teachers who have participated in professional development workshops based on *Exploring Matter with TOYS* and other Teaching Science with TOYS materials.

"It's amazing how many toys are based upon physics and chemistry principles.

Learning science concepts with toys is an exciting adventure for children. Their natural interest and curiosity in science combined with their desire to 'play' with toys provides great motivation to learn."

Jeannie Tuschl—Tulip Grove School, Nashville, Tennessee

"I really learned that there are many toys that can be used to teach science. I hope to expand the use of the TOYS concept in my classroom."

Elizabeth Henline—Mount Orab Middle School, Mount Orab, Ohio

"The toys, experiments, and activities are classroom-friendly to students of all ages."

Mary Hurst—McKinley Elementary School, Middletown, Ohio

"TOYS is a great program, with lots and lots of new and exciting ideas to use in the classroom."

JoAnne Lewis—Stanberry Elementary, King City, Missouri

"I would highly recommend TOYS for all science teachers."

Sarah Birdwell—Butterfield Junior High, Van Buren, Arkansas

"With TOYS, science really becomes part of everyday experiences and materials."

Mary White—Monmouth High School, Monmouth, Illinois

"Teaching Science with TOYS is a wonderful way to motivate children. It's a super program!"

Cindy Waltershausen—Western Illinois University, Monmouth, Illinois

"I received so many new ideas to try out in my classroom that my students will be enjoying learning science without even realizing it!"

Regina Bonamico—Chauncy Rose Middle School, Terre Haute, Indiana

"TOYS activities will enable me to help develop a love for science, genuine inquiry, and higher-level thinking skills with my students. TOYS provides a wealth of ideas to introduce hands-on learning."

Rita Glavan—St. Pius X, Pickerington, Ohio

Exploring Matter with TOYS

Other McGraw-Hill Books by Terrific Science Press

Teaching Physical Science Through Children's Literature

Teaching Chemistry with TOYS

Teaching Physics with TOYS

Exploring Matter with TOYS
Using and Understanding the Senses

Mickey Sarquis

Terrific Science Press
Miami University Middletown
Middletown, Ohio

**LEARNING
TRIANGLE
PRESS**

*Connecting kids, parents, and teachers
through learning*

An imprint of McGraw-Hill

New York   San Francisco   Washington, D.C.   Auckland   Bogotá
Caracas   Lisbon   London   Madrid   Mexico City   Milan
Montreal   New Delhi   San Juan   Singapore
Sydney   Tokyo   Toronto

Terrific Science Press
Miami University Middletown
4200 East University Blvd.
Middletown, Ohio 45042
513/727-3269
cce@muohio.edu

Published by Learning Triangle Press, an imprint of McGraw-Hill.

pbk   1 2 3 4 5 6 7 8 9   MAL/MAL   9 9 8 7 6

ISBN 0-07-064724-0

This material is based upon work supported by the National Science Foundation under grant numbers TPE-9055448 and ESI-9355523. This project was supported, in part, by the National Science Foundation. Any opinions, findings, and conclusions or recommendations expressed in this material are those of the authors and do not necessarily reflect the views of the National Science Foundation.

Contents

Program Staff

K–3 Team

Dwight Portman
Physics Teacher
Winton Woods High School
Cincinnati, Ohio

Mickey Sarquis
Associate Professor of Chemistry
Miami University Middletown
Middletown, Ohio

Mark Beck
Science Specialist
Indian Meadows Primary School
Ft. Wayne, Indiana

4–6 Team

Beverley Taylor
Associate Professor of Physics
Miami University Hamilton
Hamilton, Ohio

John Williams
Associate Professor of Chemistry
Miami University Hamilton
Hamilton, Ohio

Cheryl Vajda
Teacher
Stewart Elementary
Oxford, Ohio

7–9 Team

Jim Poth
Professor of Physics
Miami University
Oxford, Ohio

Jerry Sarquis
Professor of Chemistry
Miami University
Oxford, Ohio

Gary Lovely
Physics Teacher
Edgewood Midddle School
Hamilton, Ohio

Tom Runyan
Science Teacher
Garfield Alternative School
Middletown, Ohio

Other Staff

Lynn Hogue
TOYS Program Manager
Miami University Middletown
Middletown, Ohio

Susan Gertz
Document Production Manager
Miami University Middletown
Middletown, Ohio

Acknowledgments

The authors wish to thank the following individuals who have contributed to the success of the Teaching Science with TOYS program and to the development of the activities in this book.

Contributors

Mark Beck	Indian Meadows Primary School	Ft. Wayne, IN
Lynn Hogue	Terrific Science Programs	Middletown, OH
Dwight Portman	Winton Woods High School	Cincinnati, OH
Lisa Taylor	Center for Chemical Education	Middletown, OH

Terrific Science Press Design and Production Team

Document Production Manager: Susan Gertz

Technical Coordinator: Amy Stander

Technical Writing: Lisa Taylor, Amy Hudepohl

Technical Editing: Amy Stander, Lisa Taylor, Amy Hudepohl

Illustration: Thomas Nackid, Stephen Gentle

Photo Editing: Stephen Gentle

Design/Layout: Susan Gertz, Stephen Gentle

Production: Stephen Gentle, Amy Hudepohl, Lisa Taylor, Jennifer Stencil

Laboratory Testing: Andrea Nolan

Reviewer

Linda Woodward	University of Southwestern Louisiana	Lafayette, LA

University and District Affiliates:

Matt Arthur	Ashland University	Ashland, OH
Zexia Barnes	Morehead State University	Morehead, KY
Sue Anne Berger and John Trefny	Colorado School of Mines	Golden, CO
J. Hoyt Bowers	Wayland Baptist University	Plainview, TX
Joanne Bowers	Plainview High School	Plainview, TX
Herb Bryce	Seattle Central Community College	Seattle, WA
David Christensen	The University of Northern Iowa	Cedar Falls, IA
Laura Daly	Texas Christian University	Fort Worth, TX
Mary Beth Dove	Butler Elementary School	Butler, OH
Dianne Epp	East High School	Lincoln, NE
Wendy Fleischman	Alaska Pacific University	Anchorage, AK
Babu George	Sacred Heart University	Fairfield, CT
James Golen	University of Massachusetts	North Dartmouth, MA
Richard Hansgen	Bluffton College	Bluffton, OH
Ann Hoffelder	Cumberland College	Williamsburg, KY
Cindy Johnston	Lebanon Valley College of Pennsylvania	Annville, PA
Teresa Kokoski	University of New Mexico	Albuquerque, NM
Karen Levitt	University of Pittsburgh	Pittsburgh, PA
Maria Galvez Martin	Ohio State University–Lima	Lima, OH

Donald Murad
    and Charlene Czerniak   University of Toledo   Perrysburg, OH

Hasker Nelson   African-American Math Science Coalition   Cincinnati, OH
Judy Ng   James Madison High School   Vienna, VA
Larry Peck   Texas A & M University   College Station, TX
Carol Stearns   Princeton University   Princeton, NJ
Victoria Swenson   Grand Valley State University   Allendale, MI
Leon Venable   Agnes Scott College   Decatur, GA
Doris Warren   Houston Baptist University   Houston, TX
Richard Willis   Kennebunk High School   Kennebunk, ME
Steven Wright   University of Wisconsin–Stevens Point   Stevens Point, WI

Foreword

Science is asking questions about the world we live in and trying to find the answers. Students of science should not simply memorize definitions and parrot facts; students must be given opportunities to make sense of science by drawing connections between scientific phenomena and their own world.

This teacher resource module is not about the senses themselves; rather, it is a collection of physical science activities for teachers to use with their students to enable students to learn about matter using their own senses. Students will see, touch, smell, taste, and hear things that are part of their everyday experience. Aimed at elementary teachers, this book helps teachers provide opportunities for their students not only to explore various kinds of matter with their own senses, but also to experience the process of doing science.

Exploring Matter with TOYS is one of several books to result from the National Science Foundation-funded Teaching Science with TOYS program and TOYS: Cultivating Advancements in Physical Science (TOYS:CAPS) program, located at Miami University in Ohio. The goal of both programs is to enhance teachers' knowledge of chemistry and physics and to encourage the use of activity-based, discovery-oriented science instruction. A key feature of the programs is that they promote toys as an ideal instructional tool because toys are a user-friendly part of students' everyday world.

This teacher resource module includes 19 physical science activities written for use at the elementary level. The set uses everyday objects familiar to students, such as balloons, mittens, coat hangers, cups, popcorn, and candy. Activities based on such familiar and friendly objects will help students understand that science is part of their world. While this module does not use as many commercial toys as some other books resulting from TOYS programming, I hope you and your students find that these activities make science more interesting, relevant, and fun—both to learn and to teach.

Mickey Sarquis, Principal Investigator
Teaching Science with TOYS

Exploring Matter with TOYS

Introduction

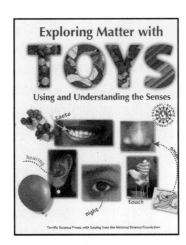

Units that teach students about our senses are common to almost all elementary curricula. These units are often taught in health or as part of a lesson on biology or life science. This book is different. It challenges students to *use* their senses while learning about them. It emphasizes the basic science process skills as a means of doing and learning science. It breaks with tradition and includes activities in the physical sciences as a mechanism to explore the physical world around us. It includes suggestions on how to integrate science activities into language, art, history, and mathematics.

What Is Teaching Science with TOYS?

Teaching Science with TOYS is a National Science Foundation-funded project located at Miami University in Ohio. The goal of the project is to enhance teachers' knowledge of chemistry and physics and to encourage activity-based, discovery-oriented science instruction. The TOYS project promotes toys as an ideal mechanism for science instruction because they are an everyday part of the students' world and carry a user-friendly message. Through TOYS and its affiliated programs, thousands of teachers nationwide have brought toy-based science into their classrooms with teacher-tested TOYS activities. For more information about this and other Center for Chemical Education initiatives, contact us at:

Center for Chemical Education
Miami University Middletown
4200 East University Blvd.
Middletown, Ohio 45042

513/727-3318
e-mail: *cce@muohio.edu*
http://www.muohio.edu/~ccecwis/

What Are TOYS Teacher Resource Modules?

TOYS Teacher Resource Modules are collections of TOYS activities grouped around a topic or theme with supporting science content and pedagogical materials. Each module is prepared for a specific grade range. The modules have been developed especially for teachers who want to use active-learning, toy-based physical science activities in their classrooms, but who may not have been able to attend a TOYS workshop at the Miami site or at one of the Affiliate sites nationwide. The Modules do not assume any particular prior knowledge of physical science—complete content review and activity explanations are included for the teacher's use.

The topic of this module is *Exploring Matter with TOYS: Using and Understanding the Senses*. Our senses provide us with a mechanism to interact with the world around us. The more we learn about the nature of matter and about how our senses work, the more we begin to understand the pivotal role our senses play in helping characterize matter. Elementary students will use their senses to explore and observe matter. They will record, classify, present, and explain their observations in a "scientific setting." This module has been developed for use by teachers at the elementary level, but many of the activities can be modified for use by teachers of older students.

How Is This Resource Module Organized?

This Module is organized into three main sections: Pedagogical Strategies, Content Review, and Module Activities. We suggest that you read the Pedagogical Strategies section first to get an overview of the unit and suggestions on how you might incorporate it into your curriculum, skim the Content Review section to get a feeling for the topic, then read the Module Activities to understand the activities in detail. As appropriate, you may wish to reread any of these three sections as you build your lessons. The following paragraphs provide a brief overview of these sections.

Pedagogical Strategies
The Pedagogical Strategies section is intended to provide ideas for effectively teaching a unit aimed at using your senses to explore matter. Suggestions are included on ways to incorporate the activities presented in the book into a series of lessons using a variety of instructional approaches. (Cross-curricular strategies are included in each activity.) The Pedagogical Strategies section in this book covers the following topics:

- **Using National Standards for Science Education**
  This subsection explains the importance of the National Science Education Standards and describes the two major categories of standards: science as inquiry standards and physical science standards. This section also includes suggestions for relating the activities in this book to the national standards.

- **Effectively Incorporating the Activities in the Classroom**
  Suggestions are included for ways to incorporate the activities into a series of active-learning lessons that include exploratory and guided-inquiry hands-on experiences.

- **Supplemental Activities**
  Ideas for supplemental activities and topics for study are presented. These activities can be integrated into the senses lessons.

- **The Science Process Skills**

  A description of the science process skills and a listing of science process skills used in the activities are included. Because several of the basic process skills in reading, language, and mathematics parallel those that are basic to science, the activities in this book can easily provide foundations for the day's or week's instruction.

- **Assessment**

  This subsection includes suggestions for assessing the Senses Unit, a science observation sheet, an assessment sheet, and a certificate which can be awarded to students upon successful completion of the unit.

- **Outside the Classroom**

  In addition to the do-at-home extensions included in many of the activities, this subsection includes letters to parents/guardians about the activities their children have done in class.

- **Further Readings**

  A list of reference books for your students is included to help you provide further reading experiences that extend the material presented in the book.

Content Review

The Content Review section of this book is provided to introduce you (the elementary school teacher) to the latest theories about how our senses function and to one of the basic theories of the physical sciences: the particle nature of matter. The material in this section (and in the individual activity explanations) is designed to provide you with information at a level beyond what you will present to your students. It is not suggested that you attempt to teach all the information in the Content Review to your students; rather, this content will help you to better understand the basic science behind the module activities. As the teacher, you will need to decide how to best adjust your discussion of the science to meet the needs of your students.

The Content Review covers the following topics:
- Particles and the Senses
- The Particle Nature of Matter
- Atoms, Molecules, and Ions
- The Sense of Touch
- The Sense of Sight
- The Sense of Hearing
- The Sense of Smell
- The Sense of Taste

Module Activities

Each of the activities in this book has been classroom-tested by hundreds of elementary school teachers who have participated in the Teaching Science with TOYS program at Miami University and its affiliated sites. Through this testing process, these activities have been demonstrated to be practical, safe, and effective in the typical elementary classroom. While you may not do every activity in any one year, we hope that the book includes a large enough selection of activities to allow you and your students to enjoy combining the senses with some of the basic skills and concepts of physical science as a means of discovering more about matter.

Each activity provides complete instructions for conducting the activity in your classroom. The first page of each activity provides the following information:

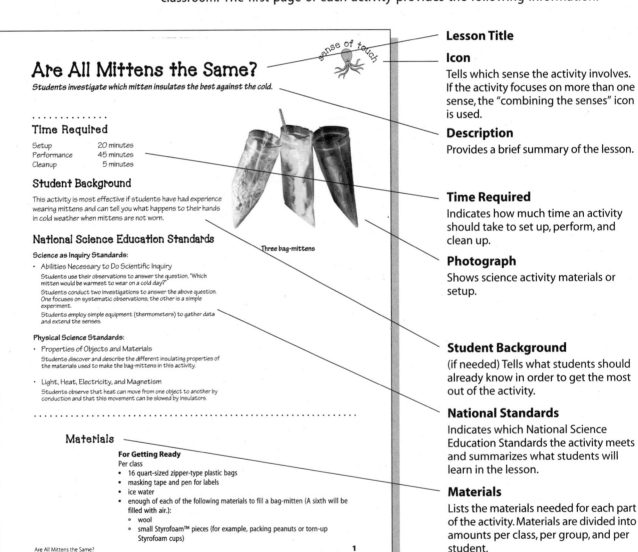

sense of touch

Are All Mittens the Same?

Students investigate which mitten insulates the best against the cold.

. . . .

Time Required

Setup	20 minutes
Performance	45 minutes
Cleanup	5 minutes

Student Background

This activity is most effective if students have had experience wearing mittens and can tell you what happens to their hands in cold weather when mittens are not worn.

National Science Education Standards

Science as Inquiry Standards:

· Abilities Necessary to Do Scientific Inquiry

Students use their observations to answer the question, "Which mitten would be warmest to wear on a cold day?"

Students conduct two investigations to answer the above question. One focuses on systematic observations; the other is a simple experiment.

Students employ simple equipment (thermometers) to gather data and extend the senses.

Physical Science Standards:

· Properties of Objects and Materials

Students discover and describe the different insulating properties of the materials used to make the bag-mittens in this activity.

· Light, Heat, Electricity, and Magnetism

Students observe that heat can move from one object to another by conduction and that this movement can be slowed by insulators.

. . . .

Materials

For Getting Ready
Per class
· 16 quart-sized zipper-type plastic bags
· masking tape and pen for labels
· ice water
· enough of each of the following materials to fill a bag-mitten (A sixth will be filled with air.):
  ○ wool
  ○ small Styrofoam™ pieces (for example, packing peanuts or torn-up Styrofoam cups)

Three bag-mittens

Are All Mittens the Same?   1

Lesson Title

Icon
Tells which sense the activity involves. If the activity focuses on more than one sense, the "combining the senses" icon is used.

Description
Provides a brief summary of the lesson.

Time Required
Indicates how much time an activity should take to set up, perform, and clean up.

Photograph
Shows science activity materials or setup.

Student Background
(if needed) Tells what students should already know in order to get the most out of the activity.

National Standards
Indicates which National Science Education Standards the activity meets and summarizes what students will learn in the lesson.

Materials
Lists the materials needed for each part of the activity. Materials are divided into amounts per class, per group, and per student.

Each activity also contains the following sections:

- **Safety and Disposal**

  The activities included in this book have in part been selected because they combine safe and age-appropriate explorations that can easily and effectively be carried out in a elementary school classroom. Special safety and/or disposal procedures are listed if required.

- **Getting Ready**

  Any preparation necessary before beginning the activity with students is listed.

- **Introducing the Activity**

  Suggestions for introducing your students to science concepts before the Procedure is performed are provided as needed.

- **Procedure**

  The steps for carrying out the activity are directed toward you, the teacher, and include cautions and suggestions where appropriate.

- **Variations and Extensions**

  This section includes suggestions for alternative methods for carrying out the basic Procedure and methods for furthering student understanding of topics.

- **Explanation**

  The explanation is written to you, the teacher, and is intended to be modified for students.

- **Cross-Curricular Integration**

  Suggestions are provided for integrating the science activity with other areas of the curriculum.

- **References**

  The sources that were used to develop the activity are included.

- **Contributors**

  Individuals, including Teaching Science with TOYS graduates, who contributed to the development of the activity are listed.

- **Handout Masters**

  For each activity that contains handouts, masters are provided at the end of the activity. Handout types include data sheets, observation sheets, take-home activities, assessment sheets, and integrative sheets.

Notes (including hints for success and purchasing information for materials) and safety cautions are included in activities as needed and are indicated by the following icons and type style:

 Notes are preceded by an arrow and appear in italics.

 Cautions are preceded by an exclamation point and appear in italics.

Employing Appropriate Safety Procedures

The hands-on science investigations in this book will add fun and excitement to science education in your classroom. However, even the simplest activity can become dangerous when the proper safety precautions are ignored, when the activity is done incorrectly, or when the activity is performed by students without proper supervision. The science investigations in this book have been extensively reviewed by classroom teachers of elementary grades and by university scientists. We have done all we can to assure the safety of the activities as written. It is up to you to assure their safe execution!

Be Careful—and Have Fun!

- Always practice activities yourself before performing them with your class. This is the only way to become thoroughly familiar with the procedures and materials required for an activity, and familiarity will help prevent potentially hazardous (or merely embarrassing) mishaps. In addition, you may find variations that will make the activity more meaningful to your students.

- Activities should be undertaken only at the recommended grade levels and only with adult supervision.

- Read each activity carefully and observe all safety precautions and disposal procedures.

- You, your assistants, and any students observing at close range must wear safety goggles if indicated in the activity and at any other time you deem necessary.

- Special safety instructions are not given for everyday classroom materials being used in a typical manner. Use common sense when working with hot, sharp, or breakable objects, such as flames, scissors, or glassware. Keep tables or desks covered to avoid stains. Keep spills cleaned up to avoid falls.

- In some activities, potentially hazardous items such as hot-melt glue guns or ovens are to be used only by the teacher.

- Students are allowed to taste food items in some of the activities. Be sure to emphasize to students that they should never taste unknown substances unless a trusted adult tells them it's safe to do so. Also make sure that students understand that they should not taste materials used in a science activity unless the teacher tells them to do so.

• When introducing an activity that involves smelling potentially unknown odors, instruct the students about protecting themselves. Tell them never to smell an unknown substance by placing it directly under the nose. Show the students how to use the wafting procedure (explained below) and remind them to avoid prolonged inhalation of objectionable odors—such odors are typically not good for us. If an odor cannot be detected through wafting, the material can be waved closer to the nose.

To smell unknown odors, hold the container approximately 6 inches from the nose and, using the free hand, gently waft the air above the open container toward the nose. (See Figure 1.)

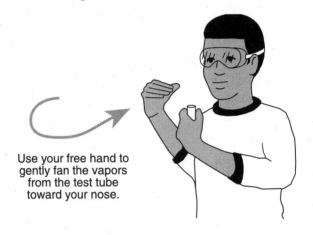

Use your free hand to gently fan the vapors from the test tube toward your nose.

Figure 1: Show your students how to use the wafting procedure to smell unknown odors.

Pedagogical Strategies

A variety of instructional approaches can be effectively used to present the science content in this book. To maximize active student learning, we have included specific suggestions for addressing the National Standards for Science Education; for developing science process skills in your students; and for incorporating guided and open-ended inquiry, learning cycles, cooperative learning, cross-curricular integration of science, and science-technology-society in your classroom. These pedagogical strategies are based on modern methods of science education that originated with theories of cognitive functioning introduced by Jean Piaget; these theories are summarized in the following statements.

- If students are to give up misconceptions about science, they must have an opportunity to actively reconstruct their world view based on exploration, interpretation, and organization of new ideas (Bybee, 1990).
- Exploration, interpretation, and organization of new ideas are most effective in a curriculum where hands-on, inquiry-based activities are integrated into learning cycle units (Renner, 1988).
- Hands-on, inquiry-based activities that involve conceptual change, problem solving, divergent thinking, and creativity are particularly effective in cooperative-learning situations (Johnson, 1990).

The suggestions in this section were provided by teachers who have used the book in a variety of ways. Some teachers used the activities in the collection as the basis of a classroom unit which lasted for several weeks. Other teachers used this book as a school-wide thematic unit on the senses which spanned several grade levels within the school and culminated in a senses fair and sharing between grade levels. This section is intended to provide you with a basis for integrating these materials into your own curriculum. We encourage you to modify the presentation to meet the needs of your students and fit your own style of teaching.

Using National Standards for Science Education

Many scientists, educators, policy-makers, and parents share a vision of education in America in which *all* students will become literate in science, mathematics, and technology. This vision has been translated into sets of standards for science education, most notably the *National Science Education Standards* compiled under the direction of the National Research Council and the *Benchmarks for*

Science Literacy compiled under the direction of the American Association for the Advancement of Science. This book is organized around the Physical Science Content Standard for Grades K–4 from the *National Science Education Standards.* The activities in this book are consistent with the recommendations of both *Benchmarks for Science Literacy* and the *National Science Education Standards.*

In your day-to-day teaching you probably do not work directly with these standards. Instead, you probably work with the required science curriculum that has been developed for your district. So why do you need to know about the *National Science Education Standards* and *Benchmarks for Science Literacy* and how this book relates to them? You need to know for several reasons:

- Your local curriculum may be based on one or both of these sets of standards.
- You may be part of your district's efforts to develop new science curricula based on one or both of these sets of standards.
- Your current science curriculum may be inadequate, and you may need information to prepare you to encourage your school system to reform the curriculum.
- You may serve on a committee to select science textbooks for your district and need a frame of reference for selecting the best materials.
- You may need to justify the added expense of hands-on, minds-on science education to supervisors, colleagues, and parents.
- You may need to justify the instructional value of the activities in this book to supervisors, colleagues, and parents who are not familiar with activity-oriented science.

In the following sections, we discuss two major categories of standards found in the *National Science Education Standards:* science as inquiry and physical science.

Science as Inquiry

When we think about teaching physical science, we often begin by thinking about content objectives, such as the following: Students will learn that magnets attract iron, students will learn that air takes up space, or students will learn the properties of each of three states of matter. But each experience students have with science investigations in the classroom does more than teach science content; it also helps to shape student perceptions of what science is and what scientists do. Thus, every activity in this book has been developed with the goal of shaping students' ideas about science and about how they can work as scientists. The *National Science Education Standards* states that as a result of activities in grades K–4, students should develop the abilities necessary to do scientific inquiry and to understand the process of scientific inquiry.

Physical Science

An understanding of the physical world is an essential component of scientific literacy. Remember that students are expected to develop an understanding of science concepts as a result of observation and manipulation of objects and materials in their environment. Every activity in this book gives students the opportunity to develop their understanding through such experiences.

Relating the Activities in This Book to the National Standards

Every activity in this book can be used to help students develop skills and knowledge specified by the *National Science Education Standards.* To help you in selecting activities and preparing lessons, the first page of each activity lists two main categories of standards and briefly describes how the activity relates to those standards. Also, the National Science Education Standards Matrix Appendix shows which standards are met by each activity.

Effectively Incorporating the Activities in the Classroom

This book focuses on how we use the five senses—sight, hearing, touch, smell, and taste—to learn about the material world around us. The activities presented in this book can easily supplement any existing elementary school curriculum on the senses or can be used to build your own unit. The activities included are intended to help you engage your students in hands-on science investigations of how we use our senses to provide us with information about matter.

When using this book at the primary level, you should focus on helping your students make direct observations with their own senses and formulate conclusions from those observations. To a limited extent, you may also wish to provide your students with more detailed explanations of the functions of the senses and of the properties of matter they are using their senses to investigate. Where appropriate under such circumstances, we recommend that you use "The Particle Nature of Matter" in the Content Review section as a guide, limiting your explanation to the simple discussion of particles as outlined in that section. We strongly recommend that discussion of the various types of particles (such as atoms, molecules, ions) be held to later years in the curriculum when the students are conceptually ready for this level of detail.

At the intermediate level, you may wish to expand your discussion to include the basic idea that our senses involve direct interaction with either energy (e.g., sound energy allows us to hear, light energy provides the impetus for sight) or matter (e.g., we smell and taste because the particles of matter come into direct

contact with our sense organs); touch can be either a matter-initiated (such as texture) or an energy-initiated (heat or cool) sense. You may wish to explain that once the initial contact has been made, a complicated series of chemical and electrical reactions occur which eventually send a message to the brain allowing us to experience our observation.

Each activity includes suggestions for cross-curricular integration. Some additional pedagogical suggestions are outlined in this section.

Webbing and Charting

In introducing a unit on the senses, you may wish to begin by asking students to help you identify the five senses. A chart similar to that shown in Figure 2 can be used to represent the senses. Teachers may choose to use the pictures provided on pages 27–32 (which may be copied for classroom use) or purchase or make more colorful labels or charts.

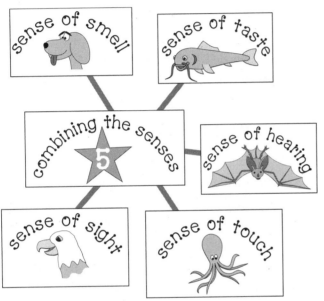

Figure 2: Make a webbing chart of the five senses.

With the five senses identified, students are then ready to consider three important questions:

- What do we already know about our senses?
- What do we want to find out about our senses?
- How can we find out?

Questions should be considered in this order, with students being encouraged to provide many answers to each. Record the responses on a large easel-sized chart so that the responses can remain on the class bulletin board throughout the unit for continual reference. We recommend that you have your students address one question at a time and that you allow sufficient time for discussion and response before the next question is addressed. Be sure that students think of an answer to "How can we find out?" for each item listed in "What do we want to find out?" In addition to acting as facilitator of this lesson, you may wish to act as recorder and list the student responses on the charts. By first jotting down cryptic notes from the students' responses and subsequently recopying into a neat format with complete sentences, the teacher can model an important part of the writing process often not shown to students.

Selecting the Activities

Which activities you do and the order in which you do them are up to you. In classroom testing, some teachers noted that they wanted to start the unit with an activity that involved all of the five senses, while others preferred to hold activities of this type to the end as summarizing activities. Some teachers chose to concentrate on one sense a week, doing several of the activities involving that sense during the week; others preferred a much shorter time frame and selected a different sense and corresponding activity (or activities) to be done each day.

Challenging Your Students

Challenge your students to be good predictors and good communicators. Young students whose writing skills are limited can still predict and communicate through speaking and drawing. Science affords opportunities for lessons on adjectives to expand the children's vocabulary. It affords opportunities for recording procedures so that the activity can be repeated at home. It affords the students a common ground for success with immediate reinforcement of accomplishing a task at hand. Science provides motivation to take on difficult challenges while helping younger children develop the concentration skills necessary to complete multiple-step activities.

Science also provides an avenue for many of the process skills found in language arts and mathematics: sequencing, recording information, communicating, classifying, etc. A list of the principal science process skills which are employed in each of the activities is provided on pages 18 and 19.

As the teacher, it is important that you avoid the common trap of being a forecaster of what to wait for or what will happen. Rather, enable your students to be involved in the process of science and to construct their own understanding. Challenge them to make predictions. Help them record their predictions, do the experiment, record their observations, and reflect on how their observations and predictions varied or were the same. By using constructivist methods, you can help your students develop the skills necessary to eventually take responsibility for their own learning. Provide your students with multiple examples of a given concept to help them develop a foundation necessary for reliable predictions. (Make sure your students are able to predict rather than guess.) Encourage students to become involved in the activity. The activities in this book provide opportunities for students to see, touch, smell, listen, and even taste as they learn how to use their senses to explore matter. The book provides opportunities to safely use our senses, including proper techniques of smelling unknown materials and avoiding indiscriminately tasting unknown materials.

Cooperative Learning

For late primary or intermediate students and older, you may wish to use some formal cooperative strategies while doing these activities. Cooperative learning has been well documented as enhancing student achievement. Several popular models for cooperative groups have been described by D.W. and R.T. Johnson, Robert Slavin, Spencer Kajan, Eliot Aronsen, and others. Although these models vary, they typically include elements of group goals or positive interdependence and individual accountability. Often, cooperative models suggest specific roles for each student. If students have not been using cooperative learning routinely, time must be spent at the beginning of the assignment explaining individual accountability and group interdependence and reviewing social skills needed for cooperative group work. Students should understand that their grades are dependent upon each person carrying out the assigned task. The teacher should observe the groups at work and assist them with the necessary social and academic skills.

Kinesthetic Demonstrations and Simulations

Kinesthetic demonstrations, which involve students in role playing and dramatic simulations, can be useful in providing an understanding of the particle nature of matter and other science concepts. The following list includes some suggestions for using kinesthetic demonstrations with the activities in this book:

- Gluep—Students simulate the cross-linking of polymers to form this semisolid material.
- Smelly Balloons—Students simulate diffusion of a gas through a balloon.
- I Can Sense You Like Popcorn—Students imitate the action of popcorn kernels popping.

Class Projects

Class or small-group projects can be used to further extend or reinforce the content of this unit. Some examples include:

- Discuss some kinds of sensory deprivation and how this deprivation affects a person's everyday life. What would it be like to lose a sense? What might it be like to have been born without one or more senses?
- Discuss the challenges a visually or physically disabled student faces and what is available or should be available to assist these students.
- Read a biography of Helen Keller and how she learned to communicate.
- Have a medical professional visit the class and talk about technology that helps restore or enhance a sense.
- Have students bring in pictures and/or magazine ads related to one or all of the senses. Make a collage (or five collages) of these pictures.

- Have students draw pictures and/or write about favorite things they like to experience with each sense (e.g., a favorite smell, texture, or taste).
- Bake bread as a class, using all five senses to observe the bread (touch—kneading dough; sight—watching the bread rise; smell—bread rising, baking; hearing—buzzer or timer; and taste—eating).

Unit-Level Cross-Curricular Strategies

- Have students keep journals about their senses. They could describe things they experience each day through one particular sense, such as sight or smell, or they could write about experiences that involve several senses at once.
- Have students deprive themselves of a sense for a class period or school day. The class should then write about and illustrate their experiences.
- Have students write a story starting with one of these phrases:

> If I were magically changed, I could smell…
> One day my eyes could see sound….
> The most horrible thing I ever touched was…
> A wizard gave me a deep, dark box. As I reached in, I touched…
> If I had a magic touch…
> If I could eat anything I wanted…
> One night when I was home alone, I heard a mysterious sound…

Science, Technology, and Society Links

In the Science-Technology-Society (STS) approach, students learn to use scientific and technical knowledge to solve problems relevant to their lives and to local issues. The STS approach encourages attitudes of personal responsibility for the environment and the quality of life; focuses on the scientific content and impact of given technological options on individuals' well-being; and provides practice in making decisions about these options, taking into account relevant scientific, technical, ethical, economic, and political factors.

The Science-Technology-Society approach can be integrated with this book. The following are ideas for linking the activities to STS issues:

- Investigate the use of various sensory appeals to attractively package consumer products.
- Form a classroom company to manufacture a product such as Corn Starch Putty, Gluep, or Paper Cup Telephones.

Supplemental Activities

The following is a list of a few supplemental activities you might like to integrate into your senses unit.

Senses and Cooking

Integrate the science and art of cooking with your unit on the senses.

Smell: Make bread or any number of possible recipes that offer a distinctive and pleasant aroma, or have students interview parents or adults at school about favorite cooking smells.

Touch: Mix dough.

Sound: Make popcorn or fry bacon.

Sight: Bake cupcakes.

Taste: Sample the foods listed for each sense.

Senses in Wildlife

Help students learn how animals fulfill many of the same needs that students have.

Smell: How do many animals use smell to find food and mates and detect predators?

Sight: How do nocturnal (active at night) animals see in the dark?

Sound: How do bats use sonar to catch insects and to navigate?

Touch: How do worms use touch to learn where they are and to avoid hazards?

Taste: How do catfish use taste to find food? (Bottom fishes, such as catfish, have many taste receptors on their skin, fins, and barbels, or whiskers.)

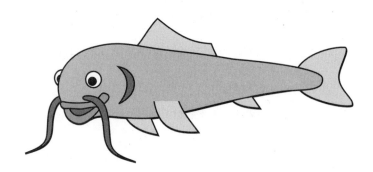

Loss of a Sense/Impairment

Help students understand the significance of loss or impairment of our senses and how we modify our behavior and abilities when we are without a particular sense. Groups of students could be assigned a certain day that they are without one of their five senses. The rest of the class would be responsible not only for helping those students with sense deprivation, but also for learning how life would be without a particular sense.

Sight: Have your students take a "blind walk" in pairs. One partner will be sighted and the other blindfolded. Have the pairs explore an outdoor area using other senses. Then have the students switch roles.

Hearing: Have students wear headphones and use some form of sign language.

Touch: Discuss amputation and the loss of touch. Have students perform activities while wearing a splint or sling.

Smell: Have students name foods they can identify by their distinctive odor (for example, garlic). Have students try to taste foods while holding their noses.

Taste: Discuss the parts of the tongue and how different parts allow for tasting. Have students try to discover what part of their tongue detects sour, sweet, and bitter tastes by placing foods with these characteristics on the different areas of the tongue. Make a tongue map showing the different tasting areas.

Outdoor Scavenger Hunt

Have your students search for items and things that can be perceived by each of the five senses.

Show and Tell

Have your students bring items from home and explain how a particular sense is used to perceive each one.

The Science Process Skills

The following list describes the different skills used in the process of doing science. Each activity in this book can be used to feature one or more of these process skills. (See the matrix on page 19.)

1. Observing · — Using one or more of the five senses to gather information. May include the use of equipment.

2. Communicating — Giving or exchanging information verbally, orally, and/or in writing.

3. Estimating — Approximately calculating a quantity or value based on judgment.

4. Measuring — Comparing objects to arbitrary units that may or may not be standardized.

5. Collecting Data — Gathering information about observations and measurements in a systematic way.

6. Classifying — Grouping or ordering objects or events according to an established scheme. Based on observations.

7. Inferring · — Developing ideas based on observations. Requires evaluation and judgment based on past experiences.

8. Predicting · — Forming an idea of an expected result. Based on inferences.

9. Making Models — Developing a physical or mental representation to explain an idea, object, or event.

10. Interpreting Data — Reading tables, graphs, and diagrams. Explaining the information presented in a table, a graph, or a diagram (including maps), and/or using it to answer questions.

11. Comparing/Contrasting — Comparing and/or contrasting different events, processes, or objects based on specific criteria.

12. Making Graphs — Converting numerical quantities into a diagram that shows the relationships among the quantities.

13. Hypothesizing — Stating a problem to be solved as a question that can be tested by an experiment.

14. Controlling Variables — Manipulating one factor that may affect the outcome of an event while other factors are held constant.

15. Defining Operationally — Stating specific information about an object or phenomenon based on experiences with it.

16. Investigating — Using observations to collect and analyze data in order to draw conclusions and solve a problem.

Science Process Skills Matrix by Activity

Sense	Activity	Process Skills															
		H	P	CV	E	MM	O	CD	M	MG	C	IV	IF	CM	DO	ID	CC
Touch	Feely Balloons						●						●				
	Corn Starch Putty		●				●							●			
	Gluep						●							●			
	Are All Mittens the Same?		●				●	●									●	●
Sight	M&M Classification		●				●			●	●					●	
	Unfixed and Fixed Shapes		●				●										
	Balloon in a Bottle	●					●						●				
	Tissue in a Cup						●										●
Hearing	Big Ben						●										
	Paper Cup Telephone						●							●			
Smell	Identifying Substances by Smell						●							●			
	Smelly Balloons						●	●									
	The Scratch-and-Sniff Challenge					●	●										
Taste	Jumbled-Up Jell-O		●				●										
	Using Taste to Solve a Mystery						●							●	●		
	Food that Pops						●							●			
Combining Your Senses	I Can Sense You Like Popcorn						●	●							●		
	A Jar Full of Mystery						●										●
	Mystery Boxes						●							●	●		

H: Hypothesizing   **MM:** Making Models   **MG:** Making Graphs   **CM:** Communicating

P: Predicting   **O:** Observing   **C:** Classifying   **DO:** Defining Operationally

CV: Controlling Variables   **CD:** Collecting Data   **IV:** Investigating   **ID:** Interpreting Data

E: Estimating   **M:** Measuring   **IF:** Inferring   **CC:** Comparing/Contrasting

Assessment

Assessment and learning are two sides of the same coin. Assessments enable students to let teachers know what they are learning, and when students engage in an assessment exercise, they should learn from it. Paper-and-pencil tests are the familiar and prevalent form of assessment. But in light of what we are hoping to teach students about both the process and content of science, traditional tests requiring students to choose one of a few given answers or to fill in the blank measure only a fraction of what we need to know about their science learning. The *National Science Education Standards* advocates using diverse assessment methods, including performances and portfolios as well as paper-and-pencil tests.

Emerging from among a host of terms describing current assessment options (for example, authentic, alternative, portfolio, and performance), the term "active assessment" has been proposed by George Hein and Sabra Price in their book, *Active Assessment for Active Science*. They define "active assessment" as a whole family of assessment methods that actively engage the learner and can also be interpreted meaningfully by the teacher.

Almost any of the experiences that make up the activities in this book can also serve as active assessments. For example, brainstorming sessions, science journal entries, data and observations from science investigations, and writing extensions can all be part of developing a picture of what students are learning. We hope that as you use the activities in this book, you will engage in many different forms of active assessment, thus maximizing the opportunity for all students to demonstrate their accomplishments and understanding.

You may find the Scientific Observation Sheet provided on page 22 a useful tool for assessing students' awareness of which senses they used in a given activity. Rewarding success is as important in science as in any other area. You might find the Congratulations Certificate on page 23 useful as a recognition of student completion of your senses unit.

References

American Association for the Advancement of Science. *Benchmarks for Science Literacy;* Oxford University: New York, 1993.

Bybee, R.; Lands, N. "Science for Life and Living: An Elementary School Science Program from Biological Science Curriculum Study," *American Biology Teacher.* 52(2), 1990, 92–98.

Hein, G.E.; Price, S. *Active Assessment for Active Science;* Heinemann: Portsmouth, NH, 1994.

Johnson, D.; Johnson, R.; Holubec, E. *Cooperation in the Classroom.* Edina, MN: Interaction, 1990.

National Research Council. *National Science Education Standards;* National Academy: Washington, DC, 1996.

Padilla, M.; Muth, D.; Padilla, R.L. "Science and Reading: Many Process Skills in Common," *Science Learning: Processes and Applications.* 1991; 14–19.

Renner, J.W.; Abraham, M.R.; Birnie, H.H. "The Necessity of Each Phase of the Learning Cycle in Teaching High School Physics," *Journal of Research in Science Teaching.* 25(1), 39–58.

A Scientific Observation

This is my observation of _____ .

1. Touch _____

    _____

    _____

2. See _____

    _____

    _____

3. Hear _____

    _____

    _____

4. Smell _____

    _____

    _____

5. Taste _____

    _____

    _____

On the back of this sheet, draw a picture of what you observed.

 Reproduced from *Exploring Matter with TOYS*, published by McGraw-Hill.

Congratulations

to

for using your five senses to explore and observe matter.

Reproduced from *Exploring Matter with TOYS*, published by McGraw-Hill.

23

Outside the Classroom

Teachers in the Teaching Science with TOYS project have found the take-home activities to be especially useful tools to involve families in students' learning. To this end, many of the activities in this book include masters for sample letters to the adult partners that can be used for take-home activities. Additionally, pages 25 and 26 contain a sample letter introducing the senses unit to the adult partners as well as a sample letter that can be used to invite adult partners to a class or school-wide senses fair.

Adult Partner Letter

Date _____

Dear Adult Partner(s):

Next week we will begin a unit on our **five senses**. Our purpose will be to understand the vital importance of our sensory functions: **touch, taste, hearing, smell, and sight** and how they relate to our environment. We will also be performing several science experiments that are related to one or more of the senses.

A few of the topics we will be investigating are listed below:

SIGHT: **Fixed and Unfixed Shapes**—The students will observe the positions of water and ice in jars to determine differences in the behavior of fixed and unfixed shapes.

SMELL: **Smelly Balloons**—The students will investigate how smells diffuse through the latex walls of balloons.

The Scratch-and-Sniff Challenge—The students will discover how smelly stickers work.

TOUCH: **Corn Starch Putty**—The students will make a special substance and observe that it can act as both a solid and a liquid.

HEARING: **Food that Pops**—The students will taste a type of candy that reacts with their saliva to create a chemical reaction that can be not only tasted, but also felt and heard.

TASTE: **I Can Sense You Like Popcorn**—The students will learn that all five of their senses can be used while making and eating popcorn.

Activities that you can do with your child will be sent home throughout the unit.

The class will be culminating this special unit on the five senses with a **SENSES FAIR** to be held on

_____ at _____ .

More information about this exciting unit will be coming soon.

Sincerely,

_____

Adult Partner Invitation

Date _____

Dear Adult Partner(s):

We have been studying our five senses for the past few weeks. As previously mentioned, we will be culminating this unit with a very special activity.

Our class is holding a **Senses Fair** on _____ at _____ .
Your child,_____ , will be performing a special investigation
called _____ at the fair. Please help practice this at home
and discuss the questions (and possible answers) that have also been included.

We hope that you are able to attend our Senses Fair. Please return the attached response form at the bottom of the page. Thank you for your help.

Sincerely,

sense of hearing   sense of touch   sense of sight   sense of smell   sense of taste

---

Senses Fair Response Form

_____ I plan to attend the Senses Fair.

_____ I can help provide refreshments.

_____ I am unable to attend.

sense of touch   sense of sight

sense of hearing

sense of smell   sense of taste

_____
                    Signature

combining the senses

5

sense of touch

sense of sight

sense of hearing

sense of smell

Reproduced from *Exploring Matter with TOYS*, published by McGraw-Hill.

31

sense of taste

Further Readings

Read aloud or suggest that students read one or more of the following books:

Aliki. *My Five Senses;* Crowell, 1989, ISBN 0-690-04794-0.

Allington, Richard and Kathleen Cowles. *Beginning to Learn About...* series; Raintree:
  Hearing; 1980.
  Looking; 1980.
  Smelling; 1985, ISBN 0-8172-2488-2.
  Tasting; 1981, ISBN 0-8172-2488-2.
  Touching; 1980.

Ball, Jacqueline A. *What Can It Be? Riddles About the Senses;* Silver, 1990,
  ISBN 0-671-94104-6.

Bender, Lionel. *The Body (Through the Microscope);* Gloucester, 1989,
  ISBN 0-5311-7184-1.

Brenner, Barbara. *Faces;* Dutton, 1970.

Brown, Marcia. *Walk with Your Eyes;* Watts, 1979, ISBN 0-5310-2385-0.

Curry, Peter. *I Can Hear;* Price-Stern, 1984.

Curry, Peter. *I Can See;* Price-Stern, 1984, ISBN 0-0066-2053-1.

Dineen, Jacquelyn. *The Five Senses;* Silver Burdett, 1988, ISBN 0-0066-2054-X.

Hoover, Rosalie and Barbara Murphy. *Learning About Our Five Senses;* Good
  Apple, 1981, ISBN 0-86653-013-4.

Leigh, Tom. *What's Inside;* Western, 1979, ISBN 0-3071-2153-4.

Markle, Sandra. *Outside and Inside You;* Bradbury, 1991, ISBN 0-02-762311-4.

Moncure, Jane B. *The Look Book;* Childrens Press, 1982, ISBN 0-516-43251-6.

Moncure, Jane B. *Sounds All Around;* Childrens Press, 1982, ISBN 0-516-43252-4.

Moncure, Jane B. *A Tasting Party;* Childrens Press, 1982, ISBN 0-516-43253-2.

Moncure, Jane B. *The Touch Book;* Childrens Press, 1982, ISBN 0-516-43254-0.

National Geographic Society. *Your Wonderful Body;* National Geographic Society,
  1982, ISBN 0-8704-4423-9.

Pluckrose, Henry Arthur. *Things We Hear;* Watts, 1976, ISBN 0-5310-0363-9.

Sullivan, Tom. *Common Senses;* Childrens Press, 1982, ISBN 0-8249-8022-0.

Watson, Jean. *Sounds, Sounds All Around;* Winston, 1981, ISBN 0-8668-3706-X.

Teacher Content Review

Particles and the Senses

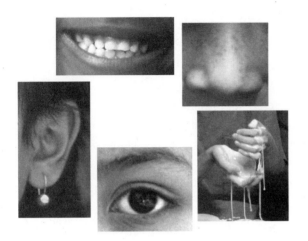

Our senses provide us with a mechanism to interact with the world around us. The more we learn about the nature of matter and about how our senses work, the more we begin to understand the pivotal role particles play in both areas. In the following section, you will discover that particles of volatile matter carry characteristic odors to our noses which in turn set off a complex series of chemical reactions that are interpreted by our brains as smell. You will learn that your very cells are mixtures of particles, and that the movement of these particles can generate electrical potentials which eventually fire off small electrical impulses that we interpret as touch. Sight and sound, considered by some as being "non-matter" senses, involve particles too. Hearing involves particles of air transmitting sound energy to our ears, and both hearing and sight involve complex series of chemical reactions involving particles (often complex molecules and ions) in the relaying and interpretation of this information. When you consider the senses in these terms, it's easy to see the important role that particles play in allowing us to live and function in our world.

It may be helpful for you to know that the five senses of sight, smell, touch, hearing, and taste are not the only senses we possess. We also possess a sixth sense called proprioception, which is the ability to know where our limbs are in space at any given moment. However, we have omitted proprioception from this discussion because it is not a sense we use to learn about the world around us.

We hope you find this tour of the senses helpful as you prepare to introduce your students to the sensations of science!

➤ *As you read this content review, you should remember that the information is written for you, the teacher; much of it is too complex for elementary students.*

The Particle Nature of Matter

All matter is made up of particles which are too small to be seen by the human eye. But in spite of our inability to see these particles, their existence accounts for matter as we know it, and, as previously noted, they play an important role in how our senses work.

The particle composition of matter varies. Some types of matter differ only in the arrangements of the same kinds of particles. For example, ice, liquid water, and steam are all made up of particles of water, and because water is a pure substance, the particles that make it up are the same. The differences we observe between the different states of water stem from the different arrangement and movement of the water particles in these samples. The similarities of these samples are explained by the fact that they are all made of water particles.

Other types of matter may be made of a mixture of different kinds of particles. Stainless steel, for example, is made of a mixture of different particles including iron, carbon, manganese, phosphorus, sulfur, silicon, nickel, and chromium. Because steel is made up of these different particles, it would be INCORRECT to say that steel is made up of steel particles. To explain the nature and interactions of matter, it is necessary to know more about the nature of the particles which make it up. So how do you know when you are dealing with a pure substance or a mixture? To answer this question, you must know something about the chemical composition of the materials you are dealing with. (When in doubt about the composition of matter, you can safely say that it is made up of particles and let it go at that.) Air, for example, is NOT made up of air particles; rather, it is a mixture of several different types of particles (78% nitrogen, 21% oxygen, and small amounts of several other gases). Based on this information, you could say that air is made up primarily of particles of nitrogen and oxygen, or more simply that air is made up of particles.

To be able to explain the nature and interactions of matter, it is necessary to know more about the nature of the particles which make it up. As adults, you have probably heard and used the terms atoms, molecules, and ions. Remember, however, that young children do not have the conceptual background to correctly distinguish between these three terms. It is strongly recommended that you stick to the use of the term "particles" to prevent creating misconceptions which will later be difficult—if not impossible—to correct. With this in mind, please use the following information as background review for yourself and do not try to utilize the information directly with your elementary students.

Atoms, Molecules, and Ions

Chemists make distinctions about ice being made up of water *molecules*, a diamond of carbon *atoms*, and table salt of particles of sodium *ions* and chloride *ions*. Understanding the differences between these minute particles of matter will help you select and interpret information to present to your students and increase your comfort level with chemistry topics.

Atoms are considered the basic building blocks of matter. There are 92 different naturally occurring atoms and a few more that have been made by scientists in laboratories. "Atom" is from the Greek word, *atomos,* meaning "indivisible." It was not until the 1900s that the existence of subatomic particles became known. Today we know atoms are made of more than 100 smaller particles called subatomic particles. The three most important of these subatomic particles are electrons, protons, and neutrons. Protons are positively charged and are found only in the very dense central region of the atom called the nucleus. Neutrons have no charge (are said to be neutral) and are also located in the nucleus of the atom. Electrons carry a negative charge and are found outside the nucleus. Both protons and electrons have one unit of charge: +1 for protons, −1 for electrons.

 You definitely should not introduce the concept of subatomic particles at the primary level.

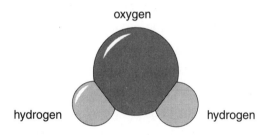

oxygen

hydrogen   hydrogen

Figure 3: A model of a water molecule

Molecules are combinations of two or more atoms that are chemically bonded together as a result of sharing electrons between adjacent atoms. The chemical formula for a substance consisting of molecules gives us information about the number and types of atoms that make up each molecule. For example, a molecule of water (H_2O) is made of two hydrogen atoms and one oxygen atom. (See Figure 3.) A water molecule is the smallest particle of water that has the properties of water. However, a water molecule could be chemically decomposed (which would require a lot of energy) to produce the three previously noted atoms (two hydrogen atoms and one oxygen atom).

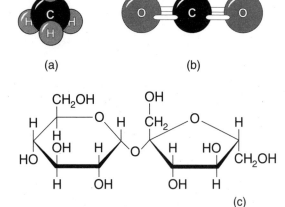

(a)   (b)

(c)

Figure 4: (a) Space-filling model
of methane (b) Ball-and-stick
model of carbon dioxide
(c) Structural formula of sucrose

Compounds that are made up of molecules are said to be *molecular*. (Ionic compounds are discussed later.) Water, carbon dioxide, nitrogen, methane (one of the principal components of natural gas), and table sugar are molecular compounds. Chemists often use ball-and-stick models, space-filling models, and structural formulas to provide pictorial representations of molecules. Several of these are included in Figure 4.

Unlike molecules, which are neutral, ions are particles that carry either a positive or a negative charge. Ions are made by the loss or gain of an electron from an atom or molecule. The charge that each ion carries results from an unequal number of protons and electrons. Notice that this statement specifically compares the number of electrons to the number of protons. Positively charged ions have fewer electrons than protons, while negatively charged ions have more electrons than protons.

Ionic compounds are made up of ions held together because of the electrostatic attraction positively and negatively charged particles have for each other. ("Opposites attract.") This electrostatic attraction results in what is called an ionic bond. An example of an ionic compound is sodium chloride (NaCl, table salt). Sodium chloride is made of positively charged sodium ions (Na^+) and negatively charged chloride ions (Cl^-). (See Figure 5.)

While the following sections describing the senses may use the terms ions, molecules, and atoms, remember that these terms are not suitable for primary students. Instead, emphasize the interactions between the particles that make up matter and particles that make up our bodies and how these interactions allow our senses to detect and characterize matter.

sodium ion

chloride ion

Figure 5: Sodium chloride is an ionic compound—smaller spheres are sodium ions, and larger spheres are chloride ions.

The Sense of Touch

We use the term "hands-on science" to describe a way of teaching that involves students directly in the process of scientific inquiry. "Hands-on" is a good way to put it—after all, hands-on science involves actually handling materials and making connections using our sense of touch.

Touch involves direct physical contact between some part of our bodies and the outside world. When we come in contact with something or experience a temperature change, receptors in our skin generate bioelectrical signals. These receptors include free ends of nerve fibers, which sense cold, heat, and pain, and special sense organs made of connective tissue cells.

To actually feel the hot, cold, and pressure sensations we know as touch, electrical impulses must pass from our touch receptors to our brain. These impulses are typically produced by a complex series of chemical reactions and physical changes. These events convert physical and chemical energy into electrical energy in different ways: some involve direct transport of current due to a difference in electrical potential, while others depend on a complex series of chemical reactions that occur within the cells. Each impulse passes from a receptor through a neuron to the spinal cord, then up the spinal cord to the brain stem. From there it passes to a relay station in the brain called the thalamus. The thalamus then routes the impulse to a part of the brain called the somatosensory cortex.

The somatosensory cortex is a kind of projection screen for the sense of touch. It enables the body to tell where each particular signal came from. Each part of the body projects its touch sensation on a particular part of the somatosensory cortex. If you could see a map of where the parts of the body project their respective touch signals, the map would resemble a tiny, distorted person traced on the surface of the brain. However, this "person" would have huge hands (about one-quarter of the somatosensory cortex is devoted to the extremely sensitive hands) and huge lips. (See Figure 6.) This map is the first, and possibly the simplest, of several skin maps in the brain.

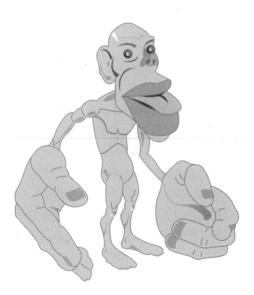

Figure 6: This distorted human figure—a homunculus—is a common representation of one of the skin maps in the brain.

The idea of the skin map suggests that the sense of touch is "hardwired" so that each circuit carries messages from only one part of the body. According to this concept, if a limb were amputated, its section of the cortical "map" should remain silent forever afterward. However, this isn't the case. Research suggests that, when necessary, the brain can adjust to use the vacant space in the map. According to one theory, the actual circuitry of the brain apparently doesn't change, but signals themselves may be rerouted in certain cases. If this theory is correct, when an arm is amputated, the facial nerves would sprout connections with the arm's neurons where they pass each other in the thalamus. Since the nerves are so close together at this point, it wouldn't take much sprouting for the facial nerves to take over. It would be like using a relatively short length of wire to hook up your phone line to your neighbor's house so you could use his/her line to make long-distance calls.

People who have lost a limb or suffered nerve damage often experience "sensation" in their missing or nerve-dead limb. Many people who have lost an arm "feel" a touch on it when their faces are touched. The experience of feeling a limb that no longer exists is called "phantom limb." Many amputees experience discomfort, or even extreme pain, in a phantom limb. Cutting the nerves just above where an amputation occurred, or even at the spinal cord, helps for only a short time, which supports the idea that phantom limb sensations originate farther up the signal pathway, inside the brain.

The Sense of Sight

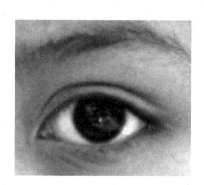

"Seeing is believing," is a phrase we've often heard and probably said ourselves. We use this phrase to mean that the evidence of our eyes is proof. But seeing is more than simply recording information—it also involves *understanding* what we see. This incredibly fast—almost instantaneous—processing of information happens in the brain. From the masses of information collected by the eyes, the brain sorts out what's important, discards what's not important, and decides what it is you see—all in a fraction of a second.

To process information from the eyes so quickly, the brain interprets visual clues based on some assumptions about the world. For example, the brain assumes that objects that are nearby appear larger and that light comes from above. These assumptions provide shortcuts that can be helpful and are reliable enough of the time that most of us depend quite heavily on our sense of sight as our predominant sense. However, when those assumptions are overturned, sight becomes unreliable. Remember the last time you looked at a photo negative of a person? Unless you knew what the actual picture looked like, you may not have been able to recognize that person, even if you knew who the person was. We need cues like brightness, shading, and color to be able to make out depth, shape, and fine details like a person's features.

Eyes accomplish amazing things on a regular basis. Not only can we see color and shape, but we can also see motion, gauge speed and distance, and estimate the size of objects even if they are far away. We see in three dimensions even though images on the retina appear in two dimensions. Our brains even correct for distorted or misleading information by erasing extraneous information and filling in blind spots.

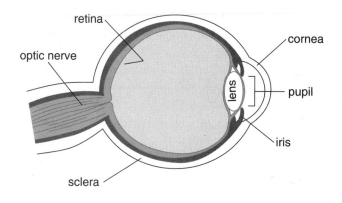

Figure 7: The parts of the human eye

The process of seeing begins with the eye, the most powerful and complex sensory mechanism in the human body. The "door" into this complex system is the pupil, the black spot in the center of the eye. (See Figure 7.) The size of this door can be changed by the contraction or expansion of the iris, the colored part of the eye. The pupil widens to admit more light when we enter a dark room and narrows to restrict light when we leave the dark room and go out into dazzling sunlight.

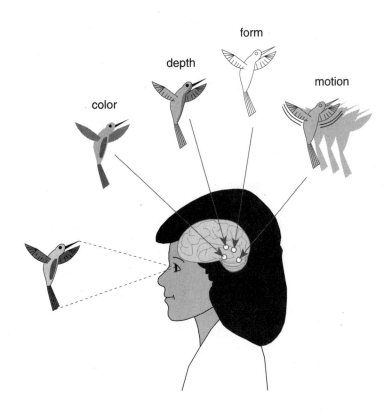

Figure 8: Different aspects of vision are processed in different parts of the brain.

Light passing through the pupil hits the retina, a membrane lining the back of the eye. The retina, which can be thought of as an outgrowth of the brain, contains about 150 million light-sensitive cells. These cells consist of rods, which respond to light, and cones, which detect color. When these sensors are excited by light, they fire off signals to the brain through the optic nerve. There are two optic nerves, one for each eye, and each one consists of about a million fibers. This number is huge compared to the auditory nerves, which have about 30,000 fibers each. In fact, much more of the brain's cortex (outer layer) is devoted to sight (about 30 percent) than to touch (8 percent) or hearing (only 3 percent).

The signals shooting through the optic nerves are relayed through the brain to a special region called the primary visual cortex. From there this sight information passes to another nearby processing area, from which the information branches out to other specialized centers that interpret color, depth, shape, movement, recognition, and other functions. No one knows yet exactly how many of these centers the brain possesses—maybe dozens. (See Figure 8.)

The presence of these centers suggests that different components of sight, such as color, motion, and shape, are processed independently but simultaneously. This idea could explain why strokes and head injuries can cause people to lose a specific visual ability, such as color vision, motion perception, or face recognition, but not other visual abilities. While nobody knows exactly how this processing works or how many centers exist, we do know that the centers usually work together to provide a fairly accurate impression of what's in front of the viewer. However, conflicts can occur when information from the eyes is misread or misinterpreted. Disagreement can also occur when a system lacks one sort of information (such as brightness) that may be needed to determine another aspect, such as depth. When the brain misinterprets what is actually out there,

the phenomenon is called an optical illusion. One kind of optical illusion is persistence of vision. If two pictures are shown in rapid alternation, they may appear to be one picture. For example, if a card has a picture of a bird on one side and an empty cage on the other, rapidly flipping the card over and over again causes the two pictures to look like just one picture of a bird in a cage. The picture below shows a reproduction of a mid-19th century toy (called a thaumatrope) designed to display this effect. (Thaumatrope courtesy of Optical Toys, Putney, Vermont, 802-254-6115.)

Besides interpreting the signals it receives from the eyes, the brain also fills in some information that it doesn't actually receive. For example, every normal eye has a natural blind spot where the optic nerve attaches to the retina. At this spot there are no rods or cones to respond to light. This blind spot is slightly off center and is big enough to blot out a golf ball held at arm's length or a person's head farther away. But we don't notice this blind spot. First of all, both eyes cancel out each other's blind spots when they are open. Second, the eye constantly moves, preventing the blind spot from being fixed in one place; even with one eye closed we have to use tricks to find it. What the eye can't fill in, however, the brain does. Instead of leaving a blank spot in the visual field, the brain inserts whatever background is likely to be in that spot. For example, if a blind spot falls on a toy boat floating in a pond, the brain will fill in that spot in the visual field with water, not with a blank spot. No one knows exactly how the brain does this, but the process may be different from simply making a subconscious assumption. It could be an actual physical process in which cells near the ones being deprived of input actually take over temporarily and broadcast their own information.

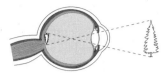

In a normally shaped eyeball, objects focus on the retina.

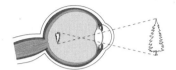 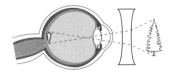

Nearsightedness: objects focus at a point in front of retina.

A biconcave lens will correct for nearsightedness.

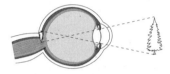 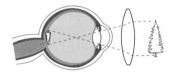

Farsightedness: objects focus at a point behind the retina.

A biconvex lens will correct for farsightedness.

Figure 9: Various lenses can be used to correct nearsightedness and farsightedness.

Given the complexity of the eye, it's not surprising that it sometimes doesn't function ideally. Glasses and contacts can be worn to correct conditions such as nearsightedness, farsightedness, and astigmatism. (See Figure 9.) Nearsightedness results when light passing through the lens is focused most sharply at a point in front of the retina, not on the retina, so the image looks blurry. Farsightedness results when light passing through the lens is focused most sharply at a point that would be behind the retina, so again the image is blurry. These conditions typically result from muscle or lens problems within the eye, but in simpler terms are often described as resulting from the eyeball being too long (nearsighted) or too short (farsighted). Both of these conditions can be corrected by glasses or contact lenses that bend the light in such a way that the rays focus most sharply on the retina itself. Nearsightedness can be corrected by wearing concave lenses, and farsightedness can be corrected by convex lenses.

irregular lens   irregular cornea   normal eye

Figure 10: Astigmatism involves an irregularly shaped lens or cornea.

Astigmatism occurs when the cornea or the lens of the eye is shaped irregularly. (See Figure 10.) A normal cornea or lens is spherical, like the inside of a ball. An astigmatic cornea or lens usually has an elliptical curvature, like the bowl of a spoon. As a result, some parts of the lens may focus light sharply on the retina, but other parts of the lens do not. Thus, part of the image may appear blurry to the viewer, while other parts appear sharply focused. Unless the eye is fitted with a corrective lens, it attempts to sharpen focus by continually accommodating with back-and-forth motion, which causes eye muscle fatigue and can result in headaches and eye strain.

The Sense of Hearing

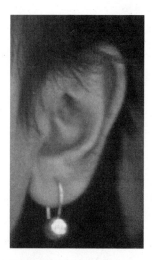

Think about the last time you listened to music or the sound of a friend's voice. Has a shout or a honk from a car's horn warned you of danger in time to avoid it? While most of us would rather be deaf than blind (if we had to choose), we do rely on hearing for some very important things—for emotional well-being as well as physical well-being. However, hearing research has received far less attention (not to mention money) than research on sight. Only recently has interest in this sense begun to increase as scientists have learned more about the fascinating, and sometimes mysterious, mechanisms of the inner ear.

Hearing is the process of picking up and interpreting wavelike air-pressure disturbances we call sound waves. These waves are produced when a physical force (such as the plucking of a string, the beating of a drum, or air traveling over human vocal cords) causes an object to vibrate. These vibrations produce sound waves, which are funneled into the ear by a fleshy structure called the pinna, which is the part of the ear that shows on the outside of the head. We usually call the pinna the ear, but actually it is only the outer part; we don't need it to hear, but it helps us to pinpoint where a sound is coming from—front or back, left or right, above or below.

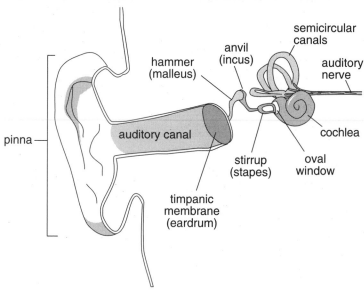

Figure 11: Components of the ear

Sound collected by the pinna passes through the auditory canal to the tympanic membrane (eardrum). The eardrum vibrates much like the head of a drum when the sound waves reach it. This vibration causes three small hinged bones in the ear to vibrate too—the hammer (malleus), anvil (incus), and stirrup (stapes). The stirrup in turn flexes the membrane of a small oval "window" in a structure called the cochlea. (See Figure 11.)

The cochlea is a pea-sized structure coiled like a snail shell and encased in bone in the thickest part of the skull. The cochlea has about 16,000 tiny hair cells arranged in four parallel rows. These hair cells are sandwiched between two membranes that spiral down the coils of the cochlea. The cochlea is also filled with fluid. When the stirrup pushes on the oval window of the cochlea, a wave of pressure passes through this fluid. This wave causes the lower of the two membranes to vibrate, which causes bristles on the tops of the hair cells to brush against the upper membrane. This brushing produces an electric current which causes a signal to be sent along the auditory nerve.

The push required to move the bristles is infinitesimal, but only a push from front or back will produce a current, not a push from side to side. The bristles on each hair cell are connected by strand-like structures called tip links, which are much like wires connecting a line of telephone poles. When the bristles are pushed from front or back, the tip links pull open tiny pores, allowing charged particles—ions—to move into the hair cell and register as a current change. This mechanical "gate" helps the ear react much faster than it could if current were produced only by a biochemical reaction; ion channels are opened directly by vibrations without the extra step of being opened by a chemical reaction. Consider that the eye can be fooled into thinking it has seen movement at 30 images a second (like a cartoon). In terms of sound, 30 cycles per second is so low in frequency that we can barely hear it, but even the ear of a young child can process frequencies of 20,000 vibrations a second (the highest overtone on a violin). The mechanical "gate" operated by the tip links speeds up the translation of signals into electricity, making it possible for our ears to process such high-frequency vibrations.

The three outer rows of hair cells have been observed to wiggle at much greater frequencies than vibrations passing through the fluid in the cochlea. In fact, these cells move at a speed hundreds, or even thousands, of times greater than any other cell in the body is capable of moving. Some researchers believe they may move in response to signals from the brain to speed up the motion of the basilar membrane (the bottom membrane spiraling down the cochlea).

The basilar membrane, about 1¼ inches long when uncoiled, decodes acoustical signals by processing different frequencies of sound and sorting them into individual frequency bands. High-frequency sounds vibrate more strongly at the base of the spiral than at the top. Low-frequency sounds vibrate more strongly at the top of the spiral than at its base. The basilar membrane is like a miniature spiraling keyboard with its highest notes on the bottom and the lowest notes on the top. The membrane processes about one-third of an octave per millimeter.

Remarkable as the ear's hair cells are, they have two important disadvantages in humans; they wear out before their owners do; and once these hair cells die, they will not grow back. Unfortunately, we begin losing hair cells soon after we're born, as they wear out from use. The ones that process high-frequency sounds tend to be the first to go. Also, over time, exposure to loud noise causes hair cells to stiffen and eventually die—bad news for heavy-metal music fans, jet pilots, and other people constantly surrounded by noise. In fact, the most common cause of deafness is the death of the hair cells.

Other animals, however, are more fortunate. In the mid-1980s, researchers discovered that in birds, functional hair cells grow back after being destroyed. Some research has shown that some hair-cell regeneration occurs in guinea pigs, but these new hair cells are for equilibrium (balance), not hearing. Down the road we may discover how to encourage functioning hair cells to regrow in humans by isolating a molecule that encourages hair-cell regrowth in birds or a molecule that inhibits hair-cell regrowth in humans. Several laboratories are currently working on this issue.

While techniques to restore hair cells may be a long way off, a device already exists that can, to some extent, help some deaf people hear. Even when the hair cells have died, the nerve endings under them often still work. A device called a cochlear implant converts sound into electrical signals and delivers the signals directly to the nerve endings. By stimulating nerve endings at different places in the cochlea, the implant can make the brain hear the appropriate frequencies. Multichannel devices, which use more than one electrode to stimulate different areas of the inner ear, provide better results than single-channel implants, which use just one electrode to send messages to all parts of the cochlea at once. Because cochlear implants pick up a much narrower range of frequencies than normally functioning ears, recipients still cannot hear as well as people with normal hearing. However, some recipients who are almost completely deaf have become able to hear people talking on the telephone. Other recipients become able to pick up a few words and use this information to supplement lip-reading skills.

Cochlear implants work only with recipients who still have functioning nerve endings. For those whose auditory nerves don't function, it is necessary to tap into the brain itself. Efforts to create such a link are aimed at a part of the brain called the cochlear nucleus, the first relay station in the brain for signals that normally come from the auditory nerve. An implant has been developed that stimulates the cochlear nucleus. However, the most this device can currently do is provide a sensation of sound; it can't make speech understandable.

The Sense of Smell

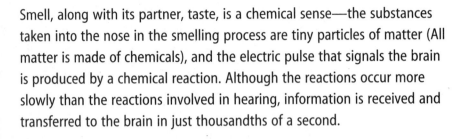

Smell, along with its partner, taste, is a chemical sense—the substances taken into the nose in the smelling process are tiny particles of matter (All matter is made of chemicals), and the electric pulse that signals the brain is produced by a chemical reaction. Although the reactions occur more slowly than the reactions involved in hearing, information is received and transferred to the brain in just thousandths of a second.

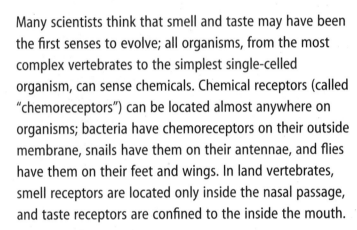

Many scientists think that smell and taste may have been the first senses to evolve; all organisms, from the most complex vertebrates to the simplest single-celled organism, can sense chemicals. Chemical receptors (called "chemoreceptors") can be located almost anywhere on organisms; bacteria have chemoreceptors on their outside membrane, snails have them on their antennae, and flies have them on their feet and wings. In land vertebrates, smell receptors are located only inside the nasal passage, and taste receptors are confined to the inside the mouth.

There are seven primary odors from which all smells result. These are listed in Table 1.

Table 1: Primary Odors	
Odor	Example
camphoraceous	moth balls
musky	musk oil
floral	roses
pepperminty	mint candy
ethereal	dry cleaning fluid
pungent	vinegar
putrid	rotten eggs

Each primary odor matches a specific size, shape, and charge of receptor in our nose. Particles of a substance fit into one or more of these receptors, triggering our brain to "smell" the appropriate scent.

The act of smelling begins when air carries particles of a substance into your nose. These particles are carried to the back of the nose, where about 5 million olfactory neurons (nerve cells devoted to smelling) wait in a bed of moist, mucus-

Exploring Matter with **TOYS**

bathed tissue. These neurons are the same kind of cells as the neurons in the brain. But these olfactory neurons don't last a lifetime like brain neurons do; they die and regenerate every one or two months. This regeneration is necessary because olfactory neurons wear out quickly from being constantly exposed to air and foreign particles. Also, olfactory neurons are unique in that one end is exposed to the outside world and the other end feeds into olfactory bulbs at the base of the brain.

Each of the olfactory neurons is topped with eight or more hairlike cilia. These cilia contain odor receptors somewhat like the ones bacteria use to "sniff out" food. The upper part of these odor receptors forms a pocket to hold odor molecules, and the lower part is embedded inside the cell. When an odor particle floats into this area, it dissolves in the mucus around the cilia and is carried into the correctly shaped receptor pocket. When the pocket takes in a molecule, the pocket twists slightly, releasing special proteins into the cell. These proteins interact with other proteins in the cell to open channels in the cell's membrane and allow electrically charged sodium ions to enter the cell. When the charge in the cell builds up to a certain level, the cell puts out an electric pulse, which passes up the neuron to one of the olfactory bulbs at the base of the brain. The olfactory bulb relays the signal to a part of the brain responsible for interpreting the signal.

The nose may contain as many as 1,000 different olfactory receptors, in contrast to the eye, which contains only three types of light receptors (those sensitive to red, green, or blue light). These thousand or so receptors are able to recognize about 10,000 distinct odors. This number difference suggests that each receptor may be able to recognize more than one smell, in which case the brain may need signals from more than one neuron to identify the smell, and thus may rely on some kind of code. If each neuron bears cilia carrying more than one type of receptor, the code may be very complicated.

What we think of as taste is really a combination of both taste and smell. See the Taste section for more information on how these two senses work together.

Not everyone's nose works the same. More than two million Americans (about 1 percent of the population) suffer from significant loss of smelling ability. This condition, called anosmia, is often caused by a head injury, but can also be caused by a gene defect, aging, viral infections and allergies, or even prescription drugs (as a side effect). Often anosmia caused by head injuries heals on its own, but in some cases it is permanent.

While anosmia is fortunately not widespread, many people suffer from specific anosmia, the inability to smell particular odors. For example, some people actually like the smell of skunk. These people may have an anosmia for the more unpleasant compounds in this odor and find what's left over to be a pleasant aroma. Smell repertoires also vary between species. For example, reproductive hormones that may be irresistible lures to one species may be completely unsmellable to another.

Interestingly, some people can be "trained" to smell particular odors. Being exposed repeatedly to certain smells may activate receptor cells. However, such training won't work unless people already have the genes to produce the necessary receptors.

Among the keenest sniffers in the animal kingdom are mice, dogs, pigs, and bears. Humans possess one of the poorest senses of smell in the mammal class; our sense of smell is hundreds of times duller than that of dogs. Unlike dogs, our response to smells is not as "programmed"—we don't feel we need to chase after the source of a particularly interesting odor. Nevertheless, smells can to some extent influence our behavior, a fact that perfume designers and food manufacturers exploit to full advantage. Smell is also a powerful evoker of memories and moods. One whiff of an odor associated with a past event can conjure up vivid memories, good or bad. And some wily real estate agents advise hopeful sellers to bake bread just before the house is shown to a prospective buyer. (Many people identify the smell of baking bread with home.)

Despite our weak sense of smell, humans are apparently able to distinguish each other to some extent by scent. For example, a breast-fed newborn baby is attracted to a piece of cotton rubbed against its mother's neck but will turn away from a pad swabbed against a stranger's neck. Mothers also show an amazing ability to distinguish their newborn babies by smell for a short time after birth. Blindfolded mothers can even identify clothes their babies have recently worn by smelling them. Interestingly, in some studies, humans have even been able to distinguish between two mice by smell.

Besides providing information about the world, the sense of smell may produce physiological effects. More than 10 years ago, researchers observed that when rats were repeatedly exposed to an odor at the same time they were given a drug to suppress their immune system, eventually the immune suppression often occurred without the drug when the rats merely smelled the special odor. This phenomenon suggests that the immune system and the olfactory system may somehow be linked.

The Sense of Taste

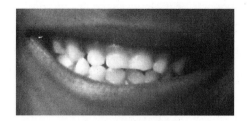

Taste, like smell, is a chemical sense. The substances that touch the tongue in the tasting process are tiny particles of matter (All matter is made of chemicals), and the method of sending signals to the brain is based on chemical reactions. The ability to sense chemicals may be the oldest sense, predating sight and the other senses by millions of years. Every organism, from single-celled bacteria to complex vertebrates like humans, senses chemicals. Chemical sensing in many organisms is essential to survival. Bacteria and many simple organisms rely on smell and/or taste to find food and avoid poisons.

Taste is one of the most commonly misunderstood senses. Much of what we usually think of as taste—that sense which allows us to savor our food and distinguish between fine wines—is really smell. When food enters our mouths, molecules of the substance waft up into our noses through the pharynx, a tunnel opening at the back of the mouth. Thus we can smell and taste simultaneously. Without the sense of smell, we would be unable to identify many foods we often think of as having a distinct flavor. If you don't believe this statement, try eating several flavors of jelly beans (or even pieces of apple and onion) one at a time while holding your nose.

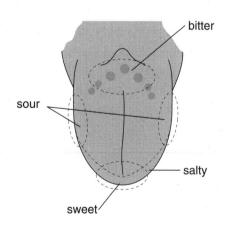

Figure 12: Areas of the tongue most sensitive to each of the four basic tastes

In all land vertebrates, the organs of taste, called taste buds, are located in the mouth. In humans, the taste buds are found on the tongue. Human taste buds distinguish between four major qualities: sweet, salty, sour, and bitter. (See Figure 12.) Some researchers also consider that monosodium glutamate (the flavor enhancer commonly called MSG) and related chemicals have a distinct taste. These four (or five) tastes may not seem very helpful when compared to the thousands of smells we can identify, but these tastes provide important basic information about the substances we put in our mouths. Sweetness is typical of high-energy foods. Saltiness can tell us if a food can restore sodium chlorides and potassium chlorides lost during exercise. Poisonous or spoiled food often tastes bitter, while unripe foods often taste sour. Cues like this help us steer toward good food and away from poisons and other harmful substances. Smell or sight may be unreliable, so taste is an important last check before swallowing.

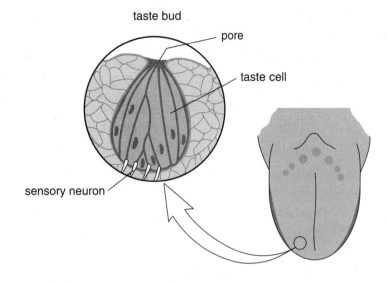

taste bud

pore

taste cell

sensory neuron

Figure 13: The structure of the taste buds

When a substance enters the mouth, molecules of the substance are dissolved in saliva. These dissolved molecules stimulate structures called taste buds. (See Figure 13.) Each taste bud is an onion-shaped organ consisting of a cluster of about 100 thin cells. These cells are not neurons (nerve cells), but they can send electrical signals and are sensitive to chemicals. The top ends of these cells are crowded together into a small pore in the tongue's surface. Molecules of the dissolved substance entering the pore come in contact with these chemically sensitive cells, which send electrical pulses to neurons connected to them. These neurons then fire off taste messages to the brain.

Taste buds probably don't generate electrical pulses in the same way for every taste. For example, sweet and bitter molecules stimulate taste cells by binding to special receptors at their tips. Researchers believe that special proteins from these receptors flow into the taste cells and start the chemical reactions that produce an electrical pulse. (These special proteins are believed to play a similar role in the sense of smell.) Salty and sour substances, however, probably bypass the receptors to excite the taste cells directly. Charged particles from salt (sodium ions) and the protons (hydrogen atoms with no electrons) that cause sourness pass through open ion channels at the tips of the cells of the taste buds. These ions probably generate the electrical pulse directly, without the use of the special proteins from the receptors.

Apparently, any taste bud can respond to three or even four tastes, but a given taste bud is more sensitive to some tastes than to others. The taste bud transmits a different code for each taste encountered.

Annotated List of Activities

The activities are grouped by the primary sense students will use to investigate matter in the activity.

Touch

Feely Balloons

Students use the sense of touch to infer what's inside of matter-filled balloons. Students learn about matter and the senses while practicing the scientific method.

Corn Starch Putty

What's sillier than Silly Putty®?—Corn Starch Putty. This activity demonstrates the unusual properties of Corn Starch Putty.

Gluep

You and your students can enjoy a fun polymer activity—making gooey Gluep! What is Gluep? It's a stretchy, slimy, cross-linked polymer that is made from white glue and household borax.

Are All Mittens the Same?

Students place "baggie" mittens insulated with various materials on their hands and predict which insulation will keep their hands warmest while holding an ice pack. Students practice the scientific method.

Sight

M&M Classification

Students learn that it is often useful to classify things, and then they practice classification with M&Ms®.

Fixed and Unfixed Shapes

Use water to show your students that solids have a definite shape, while liquids do not.

Balloon in a Bottle

No matter how hard they blow, students cannot inflate the balloon in the closed bottle. They can, however, inflate the balloon in the bottle with a hole in it. Students learn that air takes up space.

Tissue in a Cup

How can you submerge an open cup containing tissues in water and not get the tissues wet? Students learn how and also learn that air is matter and takes up space.

Hearing

Big Ben

A coat hanger and string become a sound amplifier to help students understand how sound travels.

Paper Cup Telephone

Students make their own telephones out of paper cups and string and observe how sound waves travel.

Smell

Identifying Substances by Smell

Students learn about the sense of smell and practice using their sense of smell to characterize odors.

Smelly Balloons

Students play a fun smell-guessing game while learning about how odors can pass through certain materials and how we can then smell these odors.

The Scratch-and-Sniff Challenge

Students learn how scratch-and-sniff stickers work and identify substances by smell.

Taste

Jumbled-Up Jello

What happens when two senses give conflicting information? A tricky taste test shows students that senses aren't always reliable.

Using Taste to Solve a Mystery

How can you tell the difference between four white solids that look alike? Students use taste as an investigative tool.

Food that Pops

Students see, hear, smell, feel, and taste a chemical change and a physical change while enjoying popping foods.

Combining Your Senses

I Can Sense You Like Popcorn
What makes corn pop? Students use all five senses to observe popping corn.

A Jar Full of Mystery
Where does butter come from? Students observe that milk, a white liquid, becomes butter, a yellow solid, when shaken.

Mystery Boxes
Students use several senses to discover the contents of unmarked boxes.

sense of touch

Feely Balloons

Corn Starch Putty

Gluep

Are All Mittens the Same?

Feely Balloons

Students investigate unknown solids using the sense of touch.

Time Required

Setup	20 minutes the first time the activity is done
Performance	20 minutes
Cleanup	5 minutes

Feely balloons and reference containers

National Science Education Standards

Science as Inquiry Standards:

• Abilities Necessary to Do Scientific Inquiry

Students conduct a simple investigation in which they examine solids contained within balloons and make systematic observations.

Students use observations to propose identities for the solids and appeal to the evidence they obtained to support their identifications.

Students communicate the results of their investigation by sharing observations.

Physical Science Standards:

• Properties of Objects and Materials

The solids contained within the balloons can be described by their properties, including size, hardness, shape, and texture, and those properties can be used to sort and identify the groups of solids.

Materials

For Getting Ready

Per group
• 3–5 small zipper-type plastic bags or baby food jars
• 3–5 uninflated balloons (each of a different color)

 Use the same colors in all groups. Like-colored balloons should contain the same solid in all groups.

Per class
• 3–5 types of solids with which to fill the balloons such as the following:
  ◦ rice
  ◦ powder such as flour, corn starch, baby powder
  ◦ beans
  ◦ puffed rice cereal
  ◦ sequins
• wide-stemmed funnel

 The cut-off top of a 1- or 2- liter (L) plastic bottle works well. (See Figure 1.)

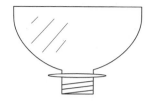

Figure 1: Make a wide-stemmed funnel
from the cut-off top of a 2-L plastic bottle.

For the Procedure

Per group
- 3–5 Feely Balloons prepared in Getting Ready
- 3–5 filled zipper-type bags or baby food jars prepared in Getting Ready

Per class
- scissors

For Variations and Extensions

❶ Per group
- 3 or more different liquids to fill the balloons with (such as water, vegetable oil, dishwashing liquid, and corn syrup)

❷ Per group
- blindfold
- variety of objects that can be held in the hand

❸ Per group
- opaque fabric bags
- variety of objects that can be placed in the bags

Safety and Disposal

The Feely Balloons can be saved for future use once they are made. No special safety procedures are required.

Getting Ready

Prepare a set of balloons for each group:

It's best to color code the balloons, for example, use red for flour, green for rice, etc. To fill each balloon, attach it to the mouth of the funnel. (See Figure 2.) Using the color code you decided on, fill the balloon with one type of solid. Do not attempt to blow up or inflate the balloon with air; you want the uninflated balloon to be tightly packed with solid. Tie the balloon after filling. Make a set of Feely Balloons for each group. (Each group should receive a Feely Balloon containing each type of solid, and each group's Feely Balloons should be prepared according to the color coding you decided on.)

Figure 2: Use a funnel to fill each balloon with a different solid.

Prepare a set of reference containers for each group:

Put samples of each type of matter used to fill the balloons in small zipper-type plastic bags or baby food jars for reference and comparison later. The zipper-type bags will not break if dropped and will allow the students to feel the contents in containers analogous to the balloons. The jar containers provide a higher challenge, allowing the students to see the contents but not to feel them. (The containers should be out of sight when the investigation begins.)

Introducing the Activity

Using one of the powder-filled balloons, gently rub the balloon on the back of one student's hand. Ask that student to identify the contents while you continue to rub the balloon on the back of his or her hand. Hand the balloon to another student and ask him or her to identify the contents. After a short time, return to the initial student and again rub the balloon on the back of his or her hand. Ask the class why the task was easier for the student who used his or her fingertips than for the one who could feel the balloon only on the back of his or her hand. (There are more touch receptors in your fingertips than on the back of your hand.)

Procedure

1. Instruct students to use their senses (except taste) to investigate the set of balloons and answer Questions 1–4 on the "Mystery Solids" Observation Sheet (provided).

2. After ample investigation time, have the groups record what they think is inside each balloon on the Observation Sheet.

3. Call on each group, asking the spokesperson to tell what the group thinks the contents are and to provide some supporting evidence for these conclusions.

4. Ask students what they might use to make the task of identifying the balloon contents easier, but remind them that they still cannot open or cut the balloons. After discussion, give each group a set of reference containers, telling them that the reference containers hold the same materials as the Feely Balloons.

5. Ask students to match balloons with sample containers and record their matches on their Observation Sheets.

6. Reveal the actual contents of the balloons by cutting open one of the sets of balloons and allowing students to examine the contents.

Variations and Extensions

1. Fill balloons with liquids (such as dishwashing liquid, vegetable oil, corn syrup, and water) and have students try to identify the liquids.

2. Blindfold a student, place an object in his or her hand, and have the student try to identify it.

3. Make opaque fabric bags, place an object in each bag, and have students feel the object through the bag and try to identify it.

4. Have students do the "What's in the Balloon?" Take-Home Activity (provided) outside of school with an adult partner. Make a set of Feely Balloons and an answer key for each student to take home.

Explanation

The following explanation is intended for the teacher's information. Modify the explanation for students as required.

Scientists often confront situations in which they cannot directly see what they are investigating. Thus, they must use experimental evidence to gather information. For example, chemists cannot see atoms, but they infer information about them through methods such as observing the results of chemical reactions. In this activity, students rely on their senses of touch, sight, smell, and hearing to make observations and infer the contents of the Feely Balloons without direct evidence. If corn starch is used, students will notice a squeaky sound when the balloon is rubbed back and forth between their fingers. Flour, although also a powder, does not squeak. Other solids, such as rice, can often be detected by the shape of the pieces projecting out at the side of the balloon.

All matter takes up space and has mass: solids are one form of matter. Solids have a shape of their own—a fixed volume. They can be described by shape, size, color, texture, sound, scent, and taste. Our senses can help us detect likenesses and differences in solids (as in other forms of matter) and thus help us distinguish one solid from another.

Assessment

Partner pairs of students. Direct each student to explain to their partner how they made their decision about which solid was in the balloon.

Cross-Curricular Integration

Art:
- Have students create feely pictures: Draw an outline, add glue, and cover the glue with one or more of types of matter discovered in the Feely Balloons. When the artwork is dry, students can trade pictures, feel them (with eyes closed), and try to identify the different materials on the picture.
- Texture is an important clue when identifying materials by touch. Students can further explore texture by making rubbings: Use a large sheet of white paper. Find textured objects outdoors or indoors. Place the object under the paper and rub it with the side of a peeled crayon.

Language arts:
- Play a game called "It Makes Sense to Me." One student chooses a particular Feely Balloon or mystery box for another to hold; the student holding the balloon keeps his or her eyes closed and listens to descriptive attributes about the unknown solid. Using the sense of touch and verbal clues, the student guesses what is in the balloon/mystery box.
- Make a class book entitled "Our Sense of _____." Each student adds a page depicting a different object that can be detected by a particular sense—possibly patterned after *Brown Bear, Brown Bear, What Do You See?,* by Bill Martin (H. Holt, ISBN 0-8050-0201-4), where students see a variety of animals, each one a different color.

Contributors

Debbie Fatkin, Bridgman Public Schools, Bridgman, MI; Teaching Science with TOYS, 1993.
Jackie Kurek, Bridgman Public Schools, Bridgman, MI; Teaching Science with TOYS, 1993.

Handout Masters

Masters for the following handouts are provided:
- Mystery Solids—Observation Sheet
- What's in the Balloon?—Take-Home Activity

Copy as needed for classroom use.

Name _____

Date _____

Feely Balloons
Mystery Solids—Observation Sheet

	①	②	③	④	⑤
❶ How does the surface of the balloon look?					
❷ Squeeze the balloon. Do you hear any sounds?					
❸ Describe how the balloon feels.					
❹ Sniff the balloon. Can you smell anything?					
❺ What do you think the contents of the balloon are? List reasons for your answers.					
❻ Name the actual contents of the balloon.					

Feely Balloons
What's in the Balloon?—Take-Home Activity

Date _____

Dear Adult Partner(s):

We have begun studying about matter—specifically solids—and relating it to our ongoing unit about senses.

The following concepts have been emphasized: Matter takes up space and has mass. Matter can be described by shape, size, color, texture, sound, scent and taste. Our senses can help detect likenesses and differences in matter and help distinguish one kind of matter from another.

The take-home kit (See directions below) includes a set of "Feely Balloons" containing different types of solid matter. The purpose of this take-home kit is to enhance the above concepts and provide an opportunity for your child to demonstrate the activity to you.

Let your child be the teacher as you use your senses together to explore matter. An answer key is provided to help you determine if your predictions were accurate. Do not cut open the Feely Balloons provided in this kit. Please return them to school tomorrow with your child.

I hope your family members learn something about using your senses to investigate matter. Have fun!

Sincerely,

_____

Take-Home Kit Directions

1. Without opening the balloons, use your senses (except taste) to investigate each of the Feely Balloons.

2. Predict what you think is inside each balloon by describing what you feel. What characteristics helped you to make your prediction?

3. Find out how close your prediction was by reading the Answer Key provided.

4. Create some "feely boxes" or "feely socks." Have other family members describe what they feel and predict the contents.

Corn Starch Putty

Students use several senses, especially the sense of touch, to observe the unusual properties of Corn Starch Putty and discover that things aren't always as they appear.

Time Required

Setup	none
Performance	30 minutes
Cleanup	5 minutes

National Science Education Standards

Science as Inquiry Standards:

- Abilities Necessary to Do Scientific Inquiry

  Students conduct a simple investigation in which they examine the properties of Corn Starch Putty and make systematic observations.

  Students communicate the results of their investigation by sharing observations. These are recorded on a class chart for discussion.

Physical Science Standards:

- Properties of Objects and Materials

  The Corn Starch Putty mixture has many interesting and unusual properties that students can observe using their senses, particularly their sense of touch.

  Corn Starch Putty is a non-Newtonian fluid that has some unusual properties—sometimes it behaves like a solid, and sometimes it behaves like a liquid.

Corn Starch Putty

Materials

For the Procedure

Per group

- ½ cup corn starch
- ⅛–¼ cup water
- measuring cup
- plastic spoon or Popsicle™ stick
- container that will hold at least 1 cup, such as a plastic cup, yogurt container, or aluminum pie pan

  A pie pan or similar wide container works best and leads to less mess.

- plastic knife
- (optional) aluminum foil
- (optional) stirring stick

- (optional) 1 or more of the following objects:
  - coin or piece of metal
  - block of wood
  - plastic object

For the Extension
Per group or class
- 3 balloons
- Corn Starch Putty
- water
- wide-stemmed funnel

The cut-off top of a 1- or 2- liter (L) plastic bottle works well. (See Figure 1.)

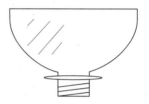

Figure 1: Make a wide-stemmed funnel
from the cut-off top of a 1- or 2-L plastic bottle.

Safety and Disposal

No special safety or disposal procedures are required.

Introducing the Activity

Discuss students' previous experiences with liquids and solids. Ask, "What are the differences between liquids and solids?"

Procedure

1. Have students do the following:

   a. Pour about ½ cup corn starch into a small container.

   b. Using your fingers or a stirring stick to mix, add ⅛–¼ cup water slowly until a gooey fluid-like consistency is achieved.

   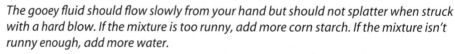

   The gooey fluid should flow slowly from your hand but should not splatter when struck with a hard blow. If the mixture is too runny, add more corn starch. If the mixture isn't runny enough, add more water.

2. Ask, "What do you think will happen if we pour some of this mixture on the desk?" Pour some on the desk or on a small piece of aluminum foil.

3. Allow students to examine the properties of the Corn Starch Putty by freely exploring the mixture. Emphasize the importance of making careful observations. Explorations may include:
   - Pat the putty with your fingers.
   - Pour the putty and cut the stream of putty with a plastic knife or stirring stick.

- ○ Rub some putty between your fingers.
- ○ Use a plastic knife to slice the putty.
- ○ Roll the putty into a ball and drop it on the desk.
- ○ Place a metal, wood, or plastic object on the mixture.
- ○ Strike the putty in the container with your hand.

4. Give students an opportunity to share their observations. Record these observations on a large chart. Through class discussion, bring out the idea that Corn Starch Putty has properties of both a solid and a liquid.

5. (optional) Set some of the Corn Starch Putty aside to examine over several days.

Extension

Make a stretch toy by filling a balloon with Corn Starch Putty. This can be done by using a funnel (as shown in Figure 2), or by holding the neck of the balloon open while someone else pours the Corn Starch Putty in the balloon. After the balloon is tied off, stretch it out and let go. Try stretching an unfilled balloon and a water-filled balloon and compare the behavior to your corn starch-filled balloon.

funnel made from
2-L bottle

Figure 2: Use a funnel to fill a balloon with Corn Starch Putty.

Explanation

 The following explanation is intended for the teacher's information. Modify the explanation for students as required.

The Corn Starch Putty mixture is a suspension of corn starch in water. It is a non-Newtonian fluid, which means that it does not behave as a typical fluid: it has properties of both solids and liquids. Corn Starch Putty flows like a liquid but breaks into pieces like a solid. It looks wet but becomes powdery when you rub it. It does not support the weight of an object laid on its surface but does not move or splatter when struck with force. The Putty tends to dilate (or expand)

under stress; in other words, it tends to "push back" when struck. (It is said to be dilatant.) Other familiar non-Newtonian fluids are paint, ketchup, and Silly Putty®.

Assessment

Have students complete the following sentences.
- The Corn Starch Putty behaves like a liquid when…
- It's like a solid when…

Cross-Curricular Integration

Art:
- Provide a scenario about a planet made of Corn Starch Putty. Have students design a spaceship that could safely land on this planet.

Language arts:
- Read aloud or suggest that students read the following book:
  - *Bartholomew and the Oobleck,* by Dr. Seuss (Random House, ISBN 0-394-8453-90)
    The King, tired of rain, snow, sun, and fog, commands his magicians to make something else come down from the sky, but when oobleck falls in sticky, greenish droplets, Bartholomew Cubbins shames the King and saves the kingdom.

References

"Corn Starch Putty;" *Fun with Chemistry: A Guidebook of K–12 Activities;* Sarquis, M., Sarquis, J., Eds.; Institute for Chemical Education: Madison, WI, 1993; Vol. 1, pp 39–42.

Sneider, C.I. *Oobleck: What Do Scientists Do? Teacher's Guide;* Lawrence Hall of Science, University of California: Berkeley, CA, 1985.

Contributors

Pam Davis, Flathead County Curriculum Cooperative, Kalispell, MT; Teaching Science with TOYS, 1994.

Mary Jo Gardner, Fair Mont Egan, Kalispell, MT; Teaching Science with TOYS, 1994.

Gluep

Students make this cross-linked polymer putty material and discover some of its unusual properties.

Time Required

Setup   15 minutes
Performance   30 minutes
Cleanup   5 minutes

National Science Education Standards

Science as Inquiry Standards:

* Abilities Necessary to Do Scientific Inquiry

  Students conduct a simple investigation in which they examine the properties of Gluep and make systematic observations.

  Students communicate the results of their investigation through class discussion.

Physical Science Standards:

* Properties of Objects and Materials

  Gluep is a kind of material called a cross-linked polymer. Gluep results from a chemical reaction that occurs when a glue solution and a borax solution are combined. Gluep has many interesting and unusual properties that students can observe using their senses, particularly their sense of touch.

Borax, glue, and Gluep in a plastic bag

Materials

For Getting Ready
Per class of 30 students
* 2 tablespoons (30 milliliters) laundry borax (sodium tetraborate decahydrate, $Na_2B_4O_7 \cdot 10H_2O$)
* 2 cups (approximately 500 milliliters) white glue

➤ *Washable "school glue" does not work well.*

* water
* stirring stick
* (optional) food color
* 2 containers to hold mixtures

➤ *"Pop-beakers" made from cut-off 2-liter (L) bottles work well.*

For the Procedure
Per class of 30 students
* glue-water mixture prepared in Getting Ready
* borax solution prepared in Getting Ready
* 30 craft sticks

- 60 disposable, 3- to 6-ounce paper or plastic cups
- (optional) 30 zipper-type plastic bags for storage
- 1 of the following sets of measures:
  - tablespoons, teaspoons, and cups
  - 10-, 50-, and 500-milliliter (mL) graduated cylinders

For Variations and Extensions

❶ Per student
- Gluep
- water-soluble, felt-tipped marker such as Crayola® or Vis-a-Vis®
- plastic bag, piece of paper, or index card

❷ Per student
- Gluep
- cup
- marble-sized steel ball or other small, heavy object

❹ Per student
- dime-sized piece of Gluep
- small cup
- 10–20 drops of vinegar
- craft stick

❼ All of the materials listed for the Procedure, except
- substitute wood glue, colored glue, or transparent glue for the white glue

Safety and Disposal

Some people are allergic to borax. As a result, care should be taken when handling. Avoid inhalation or ingestion. Use proper ventilation when preparing the borax solution and wash hands after contact with the solid. Generally there is little danger in working with the Gluep, but as a precaution, students should wash their hands after contact. Should redness or itching result, flush the affected area with lots of water and avoid further contact with Gluep.

Gluep does not readily stick to clothes, walls, desks, or carpet. However, caution students not to put the Gluep on wooden furniture since it will leave a watermark.

Solutions can be stored for several months. Shake well before use if stored for long periods of time. Dispose of the Gluep in a waste can. If Gluep is stored in plastic bags, do not keep for more than a few days, as it typically becomes moldy with handling.

Getting Ready

1. Prepare the borax solution by pouring 2 tablespoons (30 mL) laundry borax powder into 2 cups water (approximately 500 mL) and stirring until the solid is dissolved. This will be more than enough solution for 30 students.

2. Mix the white glue with an equal amount of water, allowing about 2 tablespoons of the mixture per student. Stir or shake thoroughly until well mixed.

3. (optional) Add food color to the glue mixture.

Introducing the Activity

1. Ask for five volunteers to help you build a small section of a human polymer chain. Tell the class that each volunteer represents a monomer, one unit.

2. Have monomers link arms or hold hands. (See Figure 1.) Each link represents a chemical bond. The chain they form is a simulation of a small section of a polymer chain that could have thousands of repeating units in it.

Figure 1: Monomers link by holding hands to form a polymer.

3. Show the class how flexible the polymer chain is by leading the chain around the room, weaving between the students' desks or chairs. Ask this chain to remain standing.

4. Ask five additional volunteers to come to the front of the class and form a new, separate polymer chain.

5. Have the chains move around as before. Note that the movement of one chain does not depend on the movement of the other unless the chains get very close to each other.

6. Designate one or two other volunteers to play the role of cross-linkers, which link the two polymer chains by holding onto both chains at once. (See Figure 2.)

Figure 2: Cross-linkers limit the movement of polymer chains.

7. The movement of one chain now depends on the movement of the other; the cross-linkers hold the chains together. Show this by having the chains try to move in the same direction. The cross-linkers will need to move also.

8. Now have the chains move in opposite directions. The cross-link bond must break from one of the chains. If the chains are moved back together, the cross-links can reform in new places or the same place.

Procedure

Have students do the following:

1. Measure 2 tablespoons (30 mL) of the glue-water mixture into a cup. Make and record observations about the liquid.

2. Measure 2 teaspoons (10 mL) of borax solution into another cup. Make and record observations about the liquid.

3. Pour the borax solution into the glue-water mixture and use a stick to stir until a gel-like mass forms. This gel-like mass is the Gluep.

➤ *If a significant amount of unreacted liquid remains in the cup, you might want to add a little more borax solution.*

4. Scrape the Gluep gel out of the cup. Discard the cup and any excess liquid.

5. Examine the properties of Gluep by kneading it, rolling it into a ball or rope, bouncing it, stretching it, snapping it, and tearing it.

6. (optional) Place the Gluep in a zipper-type plastic bag for storage.
➤ *Do not store Gluep for more than a few days, as it typically becomes moldy with handling.*

7. Discuss ways in which the Gluep is like a liquid or like a solid.

Variations and Extensions

1. Using a water-soluble, felt-tipped marker, write your name on a plastic bag, a piece of paper, or an index card. Flatten the Gluep and press it onto your name. The name will appear in reverse on the Gluep.

2. Put the Gluep into the bottom of a cup. Set a marble-sized steel ball or other small heavy object on top of the Gluep. Predict how long it will take for the marble or other object to disappear into the Gluep.

3. Let some of the Gluep dry out for several days. Discuss the changes that have occurred. After the Gluep has dried, try to get it to absorb water.

4. Place a piece of the freshly made Gluep about the size of a dime into a small cup. Add 10–20 drops of vinegar and stir with a stick. The Gluep will slowly redissolve.

5. Increase the amount of water in the Gluep recipe to 1½ cups of water for every cup of glue. The Gluep produced with this recipe will be slightly thinner and will flow more easily.

6. Have students complete the "Glorious Gluep" Extension Sheet (provided).

7. Try different types of glue, such as wood glue, colored glue, and transparent glue.

Explanation

The following explanation is intended for the teacher's information. Modify the explanation for students as required.

Gluep is an example of a cross-linked polymer. It is made from white glue, which contains the polymer polyvinyl acetate, and borax, which is the active cross-linking agent. A polymer is a huge, chain-like molecule made by combining hundreds and thousands of small molecules called monomers. In fact, the word polymer comes from the Greek words *poly,* meaning many, and *mer,* meaning unit. The repeating unit in the polyvinyl acetate polymer molecule is shown in Figure 3.

$$\left[\begin{array}{cc} \overset{\displaystyle H}{\underset{\displaystyle H}{\overset{|}{\underset{|}{C}}}} & \overset{\displaystyle H}{\underset{\displaystyle \underset{\displaystyle CH_3}{\underset{|}{\overset{|}{\underset{\displaystyle C=O}{\overset{|}{O}}}}}}{\overset{|}{C}}} \end{array} \right]_n$$

Figure 3: The polyvinyl acetate polymer contains repeating units.

To form Gluep, a solution of borax is added to the polyvinyl acetate solution. When borax dissolves in water, some borate ions $\{B(OH)_4^-\}$ form. The borate ions form bridges, or cross-links, between the polyvinyl acetate chains, thereby connecting them to one another. These cross-links form in all three dimensions between the polymer chains and the borate ions. The resulting gel has a large amount of water trapped in this three-dimensional network.

Cross-Curricular Integration

Business, marketing, and economics:
- As a class, discuss setting up a Gluep factory. Have students consider all costs involved in production and decide what price they would have to charge to make a profit. Students may also want to price similar commercial toys such as Silly Putty® and Gak™.

Math:
- Weigh various objects and record the amount of time needed for each object to sink through the Gluep. Is there a relationship between the weight of the object and the time needed to sink?

References

"Gluep," *Fun with Chemistry: A Guidebook of K–12 Activities;* Sarquis, M., Sarquis, J., Eds.;
Institute for Chemical Education: Madison, WI, 1993; Vol. 2, pp 81–88.

Woodward, L. *Polymers All Around You;* Terrific Science: Middletown, OH, 1992; pp 7–10.

Contributors

JoAnne Lewis, Stanberry Elementary School, Stanberry, MO; Teaching Science with TOYS, 1994.

Jane Newcomer, Stanberry Elementary School, Stanberry, MO; Teaching Science with TOYS, 1994.

Handout Master

A master for the following handout is provided:

- Glorious Gluep—Extension Sheet

Copy as needed for classroom use.

Gluep

Glorious Gluep—Extension Sheet

1. Mold your Gluep into any given shape. Consider your observations of Gluep so far. Based on these observations, predict how long it will take for the Gluep to flatten. Time it to see how close you are.

Predicted amount of time: _____

Actual amount of time: _____

2. Pour about 1 teaspoon (15 mL) of Gluep onto a piece of waxed paper. Spread out the Gluep and draw a circle around it with a permanent marker. Allow the Gluep to dry for seven days. Draw around it each day. Describe what happened.

_____

_____

_____

_____

_____

_____

_____

Are All Mittens the Same?

Students investigate which mitten insulates the best against the cold.

sense of touch

Time Required

Setup	20 minutes
Performance	45 minutes
Cleanup	5 minutes

Student Background

This activity is most effective if students have had experience wearing mittens and can tell you what happens to their hands in cold weather when mittens are not worn.

Three bag-mittens

National Science Education Standards

Science as Inquiry Standards:

- Abilities Necessary to Do Scientific Inquiry

  Students use their observations to answer the question "Which mitten would be warmest to wear on a cold day?"

  Students conduct two investigations to answer the above question. One focuses on systematic observations; the other is a simple experiment.

  Students employ simple equipment (thermometers) to gather data and extend the senses.

Physical Science Standards:

- Properties of Objects and Materials

  Students discover and describe the different insulating properties of the materials used to make the bag-mittens in this activity.

- Light, Heat, Electricity, and Magnetism

  Students observe that heat can move from one object to another by conduction and that this movement can be slowed by insulators.

Materials

For Getting Ready
Per class
- 16 quart-sized zipper-type plastic bags
- masking tape and pen for labels
- ice water

- enough of each of the 5 following materials to fill a bag-mitten (A sixth bag-mitten will be filled with air):
  - wool
  - small Styrofoam™ pieces (for example, packing peanuts or torn-up Styrofoam cups)
  - aluminum foil
  - cotton cloth
  - feathers (down if possible)

➤ *Down can be taken from a down pillow.*

For Introducing the Activity
Per class
- variety of mittens
- samples of the insulators used in the bag-mittens

For the Procedure
Per class
- 6 bag-mittens prepared in Getting Ready
- 6 different-colored markers

Per group
- 2 cold packs prepared in Getting Ready
- ice water to refill plastic bags when necessary
- stopwatch or timing device with a second hand
- dial thermometer or V-back alcohol thermometer with calibrations between 15–40°C (about 60–100°F)

➤ *Dial thermometers under the name "pocket test thermometer" (#80-070-4923) and V-back metal thermometers (#80-200-1340) are easy to read and are available from Delta Education, P.O. Box 3000, Nashua, NH 03061-9913; 800/442-5444. (Dial thermometers are easier to read than V-back thermometers but are also more expensive.)*

- room-temperature water
- measuring cup or graduated cylinder in which to measure 50 mL
- ice water in a cut-off 2-L bottle
- graph paper

For Variations and Extensions
❶ All of the materials listed for the Procedure except
- substitute different insulators for the ones listed

❸ Per class
- boots

❹ Per class
- other pieces of clothing worn for warmth, such as coats, scarves, socks, and sweaters

❺ Per class
- white and black papers

Safety and Disposal

No special safety or disposal procedures are required.

Getting Ready

Each group will receive one of six bag-mittens, each insulated with a different material, such as wool, Styrofoam, foil, feathers, cotton cloth, or air. To prepare each bag-mitten, follow these instructions: Turn one quart-sized, zipper-type plastic bag inside out and insert it inside a second bag that is still right-side-out. (See Figure 1. If you have done this correctly, you will be able to zip the two bags together.) Before zipping the bags together, insert the insulation materials between them. (For the bag insulated with air, blow air between the inner and outer bags.) Then zip the bags together. Label each bag with the name or initial of the insulation it contains.

Make two cold packs for each group by filling two zipper-type plastic bags with ice water.

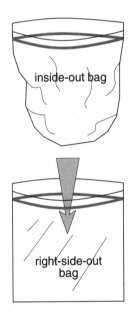

Figure 1: Turn one zipper-type bag inside out and insert it into a second bag that is right-side-out.

Introducing the Activity

Ask, "Why do we wear mittens?" *To keep our hands warm.* Pass around a variety of mittens or gloves for the students to try on. Discuss the differences in the materials the mittens are made of. Ask, "How could we determine which mitten would keep our hands the warmest on a cold day?"

Introduce the idea of a scientific investigation. Explain that scientists use their senses to make careful observations and also use tools (such as thermometers) to gather data. Show students the bag-mittens. Pass around samples of the different insulators used in the mittens. Tell students that they will be doing two investigations to determine which bag-mitten would keep our hands the warmest on a cold day.

Procedure

Part A: Qualitative Measure

1. Have all members of each group take a turn holding a bag of ice water in their hand. Do their hands stay warm, or do they get cold? Why?

2. Tell the class that today they will be trying on six different bag-mittens, each with a different insulating material. Give each group a different mitten and have them identify the insulating material in their mitten. List these insulating materials on the board.

3. Tell students to consider their experiences wearing mittens and other warm clothing while outside in the cold. Have each group predict which of the six mittens will keep their hands warm for the longest time. Ask groups to explain the reasoning behind their predictions. Ask, "How will you know if your prediction was right?"

4. Have each student in the group take a turn sliding a hand inside the group's bag-mitten and holding a bag of ice water.

5. Have students time how long it takes for the person wearing the mitten to feel the coldness of the container and record their results on the "Cold Chills" Data Sheet (provided).

6. Have the groups switch mittens and repeat Steps 4 and 5. Groups should continue to switch mittens until they have tried all six mittens.

7. Have a student in each group wear a different mitten on each hand and hold a cold pack in each mitten. Which mitten keeps the student's hand the warmest? Why?

Part B: Quantitative Measure

1. Have each group do Steps a–d with one of the six bag-mittens:

   a. Pour 50 mL water (room temperature) inside the group's bag-mitten.

   b. Place the thermometer in the water and record the temperature.

   c. Stand the bag-mitten in the container of ice water.

   d. Read and record the temperature of the water inside the bag-mitten at 10-minute intervals.

2. Create a class graph with time on the horizontal axis and temperature on the vertical axis. Have each group plot its data in a line on the graph using a different color marker.

3. Compare the curves on the graph. Ask, "Which mitten is the best insulator against the cold? How do you know?"

Variations and Extensions

1. Have the class choose different materials to be insulators for their mittens and do the tests again. Which material makes the best insulator?

2. Have the class re-examine the "real" mittens that were tried on during Introducing the Activity. Which mitten do they predict would keep their hands the warmest? How could they test that prediction? How does the best insulating material compare with the material in the best-insulating bag-mitten?

3. Have the class examine the materials found in different types of boots. Which boot do they predict would keep their feet the warmest? How could they test that prediction? Is the best insulating material similar to the material in the best-insulating bag-mitten?

4. Have the class examine the materials found in other pieces of clothing that are worn for warmth, such as coats, scarves, socks, and sweaters. How are the materials similar?

5. Does the color of a piece of clothing make a difference in how it keeps you warm? Have the class compare sheets of white and black paper that have been left in a sunny place for a while. Is there a difference in their temperatures? Why?

6. Measure the temperature of air in a bag. Have a student put the bag on his or her hand, seal as tightly as possible, and wear for 10 minutes. Then measure the air temperature in the bag again.

Explanation

The following explanation is intended for the teacher's information. Modify the explanation for students as required.

Humans produce their own body heat by eating and metabolizing food and body fat. This heat allows us to maintain a typical body temperature of about 98.6°F (37°C). Our body temperature is also affected in part by the temperature of our surroundings. This is because heat always travels from a warmer area to a cooler area through a process called conduction. Under certain conditions, the human body can be either the "warmer area" or the "cooler area." For example, when we are in a very hot place (such as a sauna), our body temperature can rise above its normal level because heat travels to our bodies; when we are in a very cool place (like outside on a subzero day), our body temperature can drop below normal because heat moves away from our bodies.

This effect of external temperature on the body in part accounts for the different types and amounts of clothes we wear. To help us lose heat in hot weather, we wear clothes that are made of light and thin materials. To minimize the loss of heat from our bodies during cold weather, we wear "warm" clothes. These clothes, including mittens, must be made out of materials that are good insulators. (Insulators effectively minimize the flow of heat from warmer regions to colder regions.) The better the insulator, the more constant the temperature will stay over a given period of time, because it takes longer for the heat to conduct through the insulator.

In this activity, the difficulty of controlling the thickness of the materials used to stuff the mittens can lead to wide variations in mitten construction and therefore in results. However, students typically report that the wool and Styrofoam pieces are the best insulators, and that aluminum foil is the worst.

Cross-Curricular Integration

Language arts:
- Have students read one or more of the following books and discuss the types of clothing that are worn in the stories and why these clothes would keep you warm:
  - *A Snowy Day,* by Ezra Keats (Scholastic, ISBN 0-590-733230)
    The adventures of a little boy in the city on a very snowy day.
  - *The Mitten: A Ukrainian Folk Tale,* by Jan Brett (G.P. Putnam's Sons, ISBN 0-399-21920-X)
    A retelling of the traditional tale of how a boy's lost mitten becomes a refuge from the cold for an increasing number of animals.
  - *Thomas's Snowsuit,* by Robert Munsch (Annick, ISBN 0-920303-33-1)
    His mother, teacher, and principal have a hard time trying to convince Thomas to wear his snowsuit.
  - *The Jacket I Wear in the Snow,* by Shirley Neitzel (Greenwillow, ISBN 0-590-43945-6)
    A young girl names all the clothes that she must wear to play in the snow.

Life science:
- Have the class study arctic animals to learn how these animals are adapted to stay warm in their cold environment.
- Have the class study how wearing clothing that is appropriate for the weather helps them stay healthy.

Social studies:
- Have the class study the Inuit people of the Arctic and examine the types of clothing they wear to insulate them from the cold.

Contributor

Lorry Swindler, Holmes Elementary, Wilmington, OH; Teaching Science with TOYS, 1992–93.

Handout Master

A master for the following handout is provided:
- Cold Chills—Data Sheet

Copy as needed for classroom use.

Names _____   _____

_____   _____

Are All Mittens the Same?

Cold Chills—Data Sheet

How long does it take for a person's hand to get cold wearing each mitten? Have one group member put on the mitten and hold the ice pack. Time how long it takes for the mitten-wearer to feel the cold.

Name of Insulator	Time It Takes for Hand to Feel Cold
1.	
2.	
3.	
4.	
5.	
6.	

sense of sight

M&M Classification

Fixed and Unfixed Shapes

Balloon in a Bottle

Tissue in a Cup

M&M Classification

Students use classification skills to sort M&M® candies by color and practice graphing.

Assorted colors of M&Ms

Time Required

Setup	none
Performance	45 minutes
Cleanup	5 minutes

Student Background

Students should have some experience with grouping, patterning, and classifying objects.

National Science Education Standards

Science as Inquiry Standards:

- Abilities Necessary to Do Scientific Inquiry

  Students conduct a simple investigation in which they use the sense of sight to examine one observable property of M&M candies (color) and make systematic observations.

Physical Science Standards:

- Properties of Objects and Materials

  Students use one property of M&M candies (color) to sort the candies into groups.

Materials

For the Procedure
Per student
- "fun-sized" package of plain M&Ms (not holiday colors)
- crayons

For the Extensions
❶ Per student
- package of M&Ms larger than the package used in the Procedure

❷ Per class
- access to a microwave or conventional oven

❸ Per student
- package of generic coated chocolate candy

Safety and Disposal

Emphasize to students that in most cases, they should not eat any substance being used in a science activity unless the teacher specifically tells them they may. In this case, if the activity is carried out in a clean, food-safe area with clean hands, students may eat the candy when they are finished with the activity. No special disposal procedures are required.

Introducing the Activity

1. Conduct a class discussion to review grouping and patterning and review the ways students have classified objects and used patterning in the past. Discuss the many variables that can be used for classification.

2. Ask the class if they can remember all the colors of M&Ms in a package. Write their guesses on the board. Take a vote as to which color they predict (based on memory) there will be the most of in each pack. Mark the class prediction on the board.

Procedure

1. Distribute a copy of the "Candy Graph" Data Sheet (provided) and a fun-sized package of M&Ms to each student and instruct them not to eat the M&Ms.

2. Have the students open their packages and group the M&Ms by color, discarding broken pieces.

3. Have the students lay their M&Ms on the Data Sheet in the appropriate boxes, count the number in each column, and write the number in the space provided.

4. Discuss results. Which color M&M is most abundant in their packages? Which color is least abundant? How do these findings compare to the class prediction?

5. Have students remove the candies from the graph and color in the boxes to reflect the number of M&Ms of each color.

6. Compile the class results into a large graph like the one on the Data Sheet.

7. Post the student copies of the Data Sheet around the room and allow students to compare individual results to the class results. Discuss the differences and similarities and reasons for using a large sampling.

Extensions

1. Have students repeat the activity with larger bags of M&Ms. Have them compare their results.
   You will need to provide graphs bigger than the one on the Data Sheet.

2. Have students study the properties of the chocolate and the coating. Discuss the reason for the M&M advertising slogan, "Melts in your mouth, not in your hands." Have them predict what will happen if M&Ms are heated in a microwave or in a conventional oven.

3. Have students compare M&Ms with generic brands of coated chocolate candy. Have students predict which coating will melt more quickly.

4. Have students do the "Colored Blocks" Take-Home Activity (provided) outside of school with an adult partner.

Explanation

The following explanation is intended for the teacher's information. Modify the explanation for students as required.

It is often useful to group or classify matter by similar properties. The matter used in this activity is M&Ms. Most of the properties of M&Ms are the same (for example, size, taste, smell). Color is one property of M&Ms that can be used to classify them into groups. In classifying plain M&Ms by color we find that the total number of candies is not divided equally among the different colors. The manufacturer uses the following color distribution in a bag of plain M&Ms: brown 30%, yellow 20%, red 20%, orange 10%, green 10%, and blue 10%. The larger the sample used and the more trials your students do, the closer their percentages should come to these manufacturer-specified percentages.

Assessment

Observe the students as they complete the Data Sheet.

Cross-Curricular Integration

Business, marketing, and economics:
- Ask students to write about the following questions: "If you could make M&Ms, what colors would you make? How would you find out which colors would be most popular if you wanted to market M&Ms?
- Have students develop an idea for a new type of candy and prepare an advertisement to persuade people to buy this new candy.

Language arts:
- Use the "M&M Friends" Integrative Sheet 1. Have the students create M&M characters in the two empty circles and use the ruled section to write sentences about how they classified M&Ms.
- Have students write to M&M/Mars, High Street, Hackettstown, NJ 07840 to get information about the process of making M&Ms.
- Read aloud or suggest that students read one or more of the following books.
   ◦ *The Candy Witch,* by Steven Kroll (Scholastic, ISBN 0-590-44509-X)
   Because her good deeds are not noticed, a small witch steals every trick-or-treat bag in town on Halloween.

- ° *Charlie and the Chocolate Factory,* by Roald Dahl (Puffin, ISBN 0-14-032869-6)
  A boy named Charlie wins a tour through a fantastic chocolate factory.
- ° *Chocolate Mouse and Sugar Pig, and how they ran away to escape being eaten,* by Irina Hale (Atheneum, ISBN 0-68-950113-7)
  Upon discovering that they are not to be guests at a party, but part of the menu instead, two confections run away.
- ° *Cocoa Beans and Daisies,* by Pascale Allamand (F. Warne, ISBN 0-723-26156-3)
  Explains how cocoa beans from Africa come together with milk from Switzerland to make chocolate. Includes two recipes.
- ° *The M&M's Brand Chocolate Candies Counting Book,* by Barbara Barbieri McGrath (Charlesbridge, ISBN 0-88-106853-5)
  Uses familiar chocolate candies to introduce colors and numbers from one to twelve, as well as sets, shapes, and subtraction.

Life science:

- Have students research how the caffeine in chocolate affects people. Also, have them research the nutritional value of chocolate, including the number of calories in a serving. Have students prepare a brochure explaining how people can fit chocolate into a healthful, well-balanced diet.

Math:

- Have students answer the questions on the "M&M Math" Integrative Sheet 2. Also have the students do problems such as Reds + Yellows = # and have students solve inequalities. Older students could find the percent of each color using the following formula:

$$\% = \frac{\text{number of each color}}{\text{total in sample}} \times 100$$

- Have the students make patterned sequences of M&Ms.

Social studies:

- Have students research chocolate to learn about its history. When was it first made commercially? What were important events in the history of chocolate? What inventions contributed to the commercial success of chocolate candy?
- Talk about the fact that candy is made in a factory. Have the students think of other products that are made in a factory. Consider a field trip to a local factory.

Contributor

Ann Veith, Rosedale Elementary, Middletown, OH; Teaching Science with TOYS, 1991–92.

Handout Masters

Masters for the following handouts are provided:
- Candy Graph—Data Sheet
- Colored Blocks—Take-Home Activity
- M&M Friends—Integrative Sheet 1
- M&M Math—Integrative Sheet 2

Copy as needed for classroom use.

Name _____   Date _____

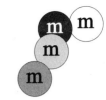

M&M Classification
Candy Graph—Data Sheet

Instructions: ❶ Lay the M&Ms in the matching color columns, filling up the bottom boxes first.

❷ Count the number of candies in each color column and write the number in the space provided.

❸ Remove the candies from the graph and color the boxes in each column to equal the number of M&Ms.

	Brown	Blue	Green	Orange	Red	Yellow
12						
11						
10						
9						
8						
7						
6						
5						
4						
3						
2						
1						

Number of candies _____ _____ _____ _____ _____ _____

M&M Classification

Colored Blocks—Take-Home Activity

Date _____

Dear Adult Partner(s):

We have been learning about classifying objects and making graphs at school. In class we classified and counted M&Ms. Then we graphed our results and made conclusions. Please help your child continue learning about these concepts by using the enclosed kit, which contains blocks of different colors. Help your child to classify the blocks by color, count the blocks of each color, and record the information on this sheet. Then have your child bring the sheet and the kit to class.

If you have any ideas to improve this activity or would like to comment on the activity, please write your comments on the back of this sheet. Please have your child return the kit to school promptly so we can use it again. Thank you!

Sincerely,

_____

Procedure

❶ Count the blocks of each color and record the number in the Colored Blocks Data Table below.

❷ Color the columns in the graph according to the number of blocks of each color. Starting at Row 1 and working upward, use a crayon to color in one rectangle for each block of the corresponding color.

Colored Blocks Data Table

Red		Blue	
Yellow		Green	

Colored Blocks Graph

	Red	Yellow	Blue	Green
10				
9				
8				
7				
6				
5				
4				
3				
2				
1				

Name _____   Date _____

M&M Classification

M&M Friends—Integrative Sheet 1

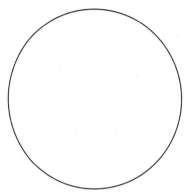

Draw some friends for Mr. M&M in the circles!

Write some sentences about how you classified M&Ms.

_____

_____

_____

_____

_____

M&M Classification

M&M Math—Integrative Sheet 2

Which color of M&Ms was most common? Color this M&M that color and write the number of M&Ms of that color on the line beside it.

m _____

Which color was second most common? Color this M&M and write the number of M&Ms of this color beside it.

m _____

Which color was third most common? Color this M&M and write the number of M&Ms of this color beside it.

m _____

Which color was fourth most common? Color this M&M and write the number of M&Ms of this color beside it.

m _____

Which color was fifth most common? Color this M&M and write the number of M&Ms of this color beside it.

m _____

Which color was least common? Color this M&M and write the number of M&Ms of this color beside it.

m _____

Fixed and Unfixed Shapes

Students predict and observe the shapes of liquids and solids under various conditions.

Time Required

Setup	5–10 minutes
Performance	15–30 minutes
Cleanup	5 minutes

National Science Education Standards

Science as Inquiry Standards:

- Abilities Necessary to Do Scientific Inquiry

  Students conduct a simple investigation in which they examine the properties of liquids and solids in jars and make systematic observations.

Physical Science Standards:

- Properties of Objects and Materials

  Two of the three states of matter are liquids and solids. Students use their sense of sight to observe that liquids do not have a fixed shape, while solids do.

  Students use the properties of solids and liquids to sort materials used in the activity into two groups: fixed shapes and unfixed shapes.

Jars containing fixed and unfixed shapes

Materials

For Getting Ready
Per class
- food color
- water
- small ice cubes, ice chips, or snow
- access to a freezer
- 3 clear plastic jars with lids, such as peanut butter jars

For Introducing the Activity
Per class
- pencil
- water
- tall, thin container
- large, flat dish

For the Procedure

Per class

- jars prepared in Getting Ready
- (optional) additional small jars or clear plastic vials with caps
- (optional) colored chalk

For Variations and Extensions

❶ Per class

- jar of colored water from the Procedure
- little boat that fits in the jar

❷ Per class

- molds of various sizes and shapes
- Kool-Aid®
- water

Safety and Disposal

No special safety or disposal procedures are required.

Getting Ready

1. Half-fill a jar with water, add a few drops of food color, and put the lid on.

2. Half-fill a second jar with water, add a few drops of food color, and freeze the water with the lid off the jar. After the water is completely frozen, place the lid back on the jar.

3. Prepare several small ice cubes, some ice chips, or snow (colored with food color for visibility if desired). Half-fill a third jar with the ice cubes, chips, or snow.

Introducing the Activity

Pour some water into a tall, thin container. Then, pour the same water into a large, flat dish. Ask the students to describe what happened to the shape of the water. Next, put a pencil in the tall, thin container and then in the flat dish. Ask the students to describe what happened to the shape of the pencil. Use the different behavior of the pencil and the water to distinguish between a solid and a liquid. (Solids have a definite shape, while liquids do not. Liquids take the shape of their container.)

Procedure

Part A: Liquid Water

1. Show students the jar of liquid colored water. Have students describe what they see.

2. Set the jar of water on the table and draw a picture of the jar and its contents on the blackboard. Label the water and the air. (See Figure 1.)

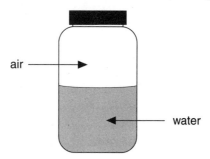

Figure 1: Draw a picture of the jar and its contents on the board.

3. On the blackboard, sketch the empty jars in the four different positions shown on the "Where Does the Water Go?" Data Sheet (provided).

4. Without picking up the jar, ask students to imagine the jar of water in each position on their Data Sheet. Challenge them to predict and draw the position of the water line of the jar in these different positions.

Students can check their own pictures during Steps 5 and 6, or you may want to collect drawings at this point to check for understanding.

5. After students complete their drawings, hold the jar of colored water next to each picture on the board to demonstrate the location of the water. Then sketch the water line in each jar (using colored chalk if available).

6. (optional) If enough jars are available, give each student a jar or vial of water and allow students to manipulate the jars to check their findings. Encourage them to test different jar positions.

Part B: Solid Water

1. Show students the jar containing ice cubes, ice chips, or snow. Have students describe what they see and describe all the ways the contents of this jar differ from the contents of the water jar.

2. Repeat Part A, Steps 2–6, using the jar of ice cubes, ice chips, or snow.

3. Bring out the jar of frozen water prepared in Getting Ready, Step 2. Explain to the students how the jar of water was prepared.

Use the frozen water as soon as possible after removing it from the freezer. If the ice begins to melt, the solid block of ice may slide down when the jar is inverted.

4. Repeat Part A, Steps 2–6, using the jar of frozen water.

5. Challenge students to form a hypothesis that explains the differences observed in the three jars.

6. (optional) With the jar inverted, allow the ice to begin melting and observe as the ice block falls to the "bottom" of the jar.

Variations and Extensions

1. Ask the students what they think will happen to the water in Part A if the jar is put on its side and rolled. Float a little boat on the water in the jar before rolling the jar.

2. Make Kool-Aid according to the directions on the package. Pour it into molds of different sizes and shapes. Freeze the Kool-Aid. Remove the Kool-Aid cubes from their molds and note that a solid has a definite shape. Have the students use the sense of taste to enjoy Kool-Aid ice cubes.

Explanation

The following explanation is intended for the teacher's information. Modify the explanation for students as required.

Liquids take the shape of the container they are in and, due to gravity, fill the bottom of a container before the upper levels can be filled. In Part A, when the jar is in its original position (with the base of the jar on the table) the water conforms to the bottom half of the jar, and its surface is level and horizontal to the ground across most of its surface. You might observe the very slight upward curve of the water at the sides of the jar, which is a result of the attraction of water to plastic. (A similar but more pronounced curve can be noted in glass containers.) As you tilt the jar, the liquid water shifts to remain on the new "bottom" of the jar and conforms to its shape. In liquid water, the water particles can slip and slide past each other. This allows liquid water to flow to conform to the shape of the container. (See Figure 2.)

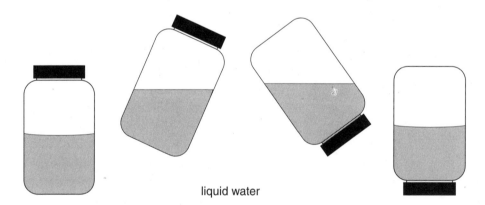

liquid water

Figure 2: Liquids take the shape of the container they are in and fill the bottom of a container before the upper levels can be filled.

Unlike liquids, solids have their own characteristic shapes and do not take the shape of the container they are in. This is readily apparent if ice cubes are used in Part B. As long as they remain frozen, the individual ice cubes retain their shape. When you rotate the jar, the ice cubes fall to the new "bottom." (See Figure 3.) However, unlike liquid water, the ice cubes do not flow to conform to the jar's shape nor do they have a horizontal water line. If you use ice chips or snow, the individual shapes of the solids are more difficult to see because they are so small.

Still, the small pieces do have their own shapes. The water particles that make up the ice or snow are fixed in a given position within the crystals. These particles cannot move past one another (they cannot flow), so a solid has a fixed shape.

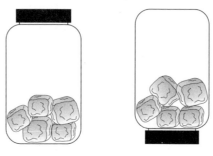

ice cubes

Figure 3: Solids have their own characteristic shapes
and do not take the shape of the container they are in.

When the activity is repeated with the water that was frozen directly in the jar, the ice does not shift as the container moves. In fact, unless the ice has begun to melt around the walls of the jar, it will stay in the same location, seeming to defy density and gravity when the jar is inverted. (See Figure 4.) This observation may at first be surprising until you consider what happens when you make ice cubes at home (assuming you have ice cube trays and not an automatic ice maker). When water freezes, it expands. This causes ice cubes to stick to the tray even when inverted; often the tray must be struck or twisted to dislodge the ice cubes. The same is true for the ice that was frozen in the jar. As water freezes, it expands to a greater volume than liquid water. This is because ice is less dense than liquid water. (This fact is easily observed by placing ice into a glass of water. The ice floats.) This expansion often lodges the ice firmly into the original position, holding the ice in place; however, once the ice begins to melt, the liquid at the edges runs down and the piece of ice slides down the walls.

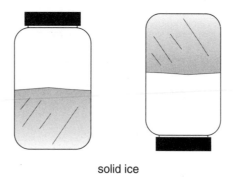

solid ice

Figure 4: Ice that is frozen directly in the jar
does not shift as the container moves.

Assessment

Construct a large chart for the class with separate columns for "fixed" and "unfixed" shapes. Have students bring in or cut out pictures from magazines that show examples of each. Let students classify all the pictures and place them in their proper columns on the chart.

Cross-Curricular Integration

Art:
• Ask students to draw pictures to answer the following question: "If someone sent you a jar full of something, what would you like it to be?" Have each student draw the contents of his or her jar with the jar in various positions, as in the Procedure.

Language arts:
• Read aloud or have students read the following book:
   ○ *Whale Is Stuck,* by Karen Hayles (Simon & Schuster, ISBN 0-671-86587-0).
   In this story, Whale jumps out of the water and becomes stuck on an ice floe. After numerous attempts by his friends to help him, the ice melts and Whale is again free.

Contributors

Teressa Jacobs, Mt. Airy School, Cincinnati, OH; Teaching Science with TOYS, 1993–94.

Mary Jane Kendall, Sherwood Elementary School, Cincinnati, OH; Teaching Science with TOYS, 1989–90.

Ann Veith, Rosedale Elementary School, Middletown, OH; Teaching Science with TOYS, 1991–92.

Handout Master

A master for the following handout is provided:
• Where Does the Water Go?—Data Sheet
Copy as needed for classroom use.

Name _____   Date_____

Fixed and Unfixed Shapes
Where Does the Water Go?—Data Sheet

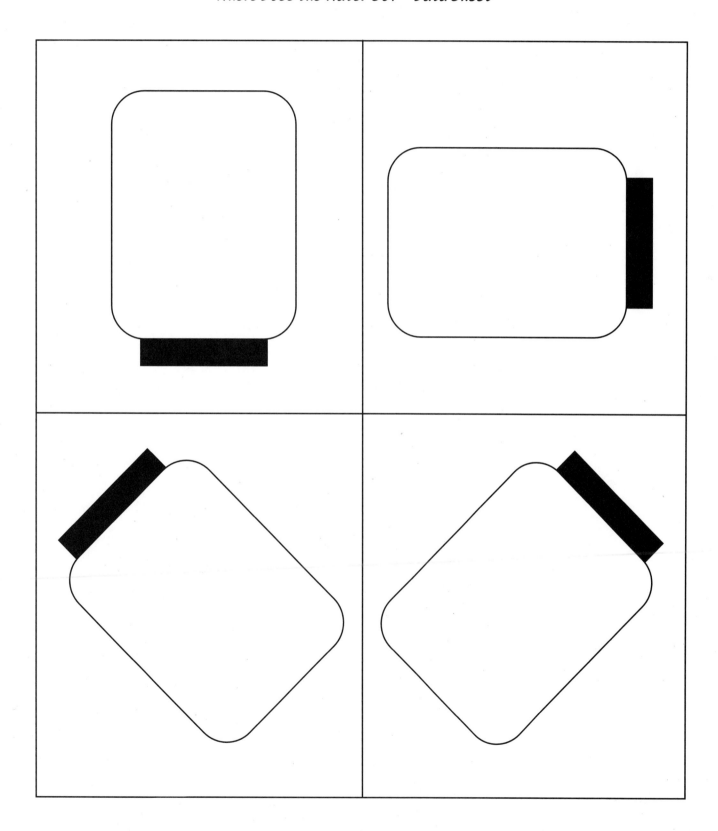

Balloon in a Bottle

Students discover that air takes up space.

sense of sight

Time Required

Setup	5 minutes
Performance	10 minutes
Cleanup	none

National Science Education Standards

Science as Inquiry Standards:

• Abilities Necessary to Do Scientific Inquiry

Students use observations to construct a reasonable explanation for the behavior of the balloon in a bottle and appeal to the evidence they obtained to support their explanation.

Physical Science Standards:

• Properties of Objects and Materials

One of the three states of matter is the gas state. Students observe that the gases that make up air are not visible, yet they take up space.

A balloon in a bottle

Materials

For Getting Ready
Per class

The sharp object, intended for teacher use only, is needed to make holes in some of the soft-drink bottles the first time the activity is done.

• sharp object such as a pushpin, thumbtack, or nail
• several balloons
• several clear plastic 1-liter (L) soft-drink bottles

Although 1-L bottles work best, 2-L bottles can be substituted.

For Introducing the Activity
Per class
• balloon
• paper bag, beach ball, or inner tube

For the Procedure
Part A, per group
• balloon and bottle setup without hole prepared in Getting Ready
• (optional) several clean balloons

Part B, per group
- balloon and bottle setup with hole prepared in Getting Ready

For Variations and Extensions
❷ All of the materials listed for the Procedure plus the following:
- water
- bucket
- hot soldering iron, hot-melt glue gun, or hot nail with a hot pad to make hole
- rubber stopper to fit the hole (See Figure 2.)

Safety and Disposal

For health reasons, use a clean balloon for each student. Use caution with items needed to make holes in the bottles. No special disposal procedures are required.

Getting Ready

1. For Part A, make a balloon in a bottle setup without a hole for each group: Push a deflated balloon into a bottle (without a hole) and stretch the open end of the balloon back over the bottle's mouth to seal the bottle. (See Figure 1.)

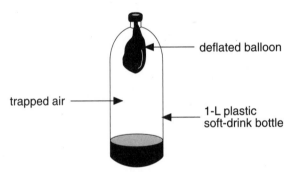

deflated balloon

trapped air

1-L plastic
soft-drink bottle

Figure 1: Prepare the balloon in a bottle.

2. For Part B, make a balloon in a bottle setup with a hole for each group: Put a hole in a plastic bottle by carefully pushing a pushpin, thumbtack, or nail through the side. Insert a balloon as before.

Introducing the Activity

Blow up a balloon in front of the class and discuss how the balloon expands as air is pushed into it during the blowing process. Tie off the balloon and gently squeeze it to show that the balloon cannot be completely flattened without popping it. Ask students to propose explanations. Accept and record all ideas, but don't tell them the answer yet. (Blowing up a balloon is an example of air taking up space.) You may want to pop the balloon to show it can indeed be flattened. To further illustrate the fact that air takes up space, blow up other items (such as a paper bag, beach ball, or inner tube).

Procedure

Part A: The Challenge

As an alternative to this Procedure, set up the activity at a learning center and let students do the Procedure with "The Air in There" Data Sheet (provided).

1. Divide the class into groups. Let each group select a representative who will blow up the balloon in Step 4.

2. Distribute a balloon and bottle setup without the hole to each representative.

3. Ask the groups to predict what will happen when their representative tries to blow up the balloon in the bottle. Groups should record their predictions.

In Step 4, do not let students try so hard to blow up the balloons that they become ill.

4. Challenge each group representative to blow up the balloon inside the group's bottle, and have him or her describe to the group the resistance felt when trying to blow up the balloon. Other members of the group should describe what they see.

No matter how hard the students try, the balloons will not inflate very much.

For very young students, monitor closely as they try to blow up the balloons. There is a danger that students might inhale instead of blow and get the balloon stuck in the windpipe.

5. Have each representative remove the balloon from the bottle and blow it up to show the balloon can be inflated.

6. Have the groups propose explanations of their observations and support their proposed explanations with evidence. Accept and record all ideas.

7. (optional) Give a fresh balloon to each member of each group. Show students how to stretch the open end of the balloon back over the bottle's mouth. Allow all students to try their luck at the challenge. After each trial encourage the groups to reconsider their explanations to allow for refinement based on multiple trials.

Part B: The Hole

As an alternative to this Procedure, set up the activity at a learning center and let students do the Procedure with "The Air in There" Data Sheet (provided).

1. Distribute the balloon and bottle setups with holes that were prepared in Getting Ready and point out that these bottles have holes in them. Repeat Part A, Steps 3–7, and challenge students to explain the difference between the observations in these two parts. *The balloon will inflate in the bottle with a hole because the air is no longer trapped inside the bottle.*

2. Have each representative try putting a finger over the hole before blowing. (Once again, the trapped air prevents the balloon from being blown up very much.)

3. Have each representative blow up the balloon with the hole open. (The balloon inflates.) Have each keep his or her mouth over the balloon opening. Will the balloon stay inflated? *Yes, as long as the mouth is sealing in the air.* Have each representative place a finger over the hole and remove his or her mouth but keep the finger over the hole. What happens? *The balloon stays inflated.*

4. Have each group review their proposed explanation from Part A, Step 6. Ask, "Do the results of Part B support your original idea? Why or why not?" Give students an opportunity to revise explanations if needed.

Variations and Extensions

1. Put a balloon inside a plastic 2-L bottle without a hole as in Figure 1. Squeeze the bottle firmly, and the balloon will be pushed out of the bottle and inflate partially or even come off the bottle.

2. Make a balloon water-shooter:

    a. Make a hole approximately 1 centimeter (cm) in diameter in the side of a 1- or 2-L bottle just above the base. (See Figure 2a.)

    A hot nail, a hot soldering iron without solder, or a hot-melt glue gun without glue can be used to melt a smooth hole in the bottle which will be easily sealed with a stopper.

    b. Put a balloon in the bottle and stretch the open end of the balloon back over the bottle's mouth.

    c. Blow up the balloon. (See Figure 2b.) With your mouth still in place and the balloon still inflated, plug the hole with the stopper. (See Figure 2c.) Remove your mouth and the balloon will stay inflated. (See the photo on the first page of this activity.)

    The bottle may collapse slightly around the balloon when you remove your mouth, or the balloon may slightly shrink. This will not affect the success of the water-shooter.

    d. Fill the balloon with water. Go outside (where spilled water will not matter) and set up a bucket as a target.

    e. Aim the bottle at the target and take the stopper out. Water will be pushed out of the balloon.

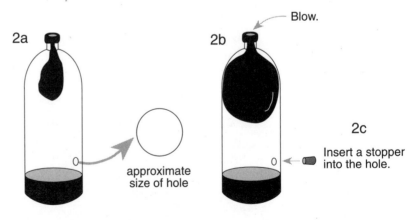

Figure 2: Make a balloon water-shooter.

Explanation

> *The following explanation is intended for the teacher's information. Modify the explanation for students as required.*

Blowing up a balloon involves forcing additional air into the balloon. The gas particles blown into the balloon hit the inside walls of the balloon, creating enough pressure to force the rubber of the balloon to expand and the balloon to inflate. The impact of these particles on the walls creates the pressure inside the balloon. There is also pressure outside the balloon (atmospheric pressure). Atmospheric pressure is a result of molecules of gas in the atmosphere pushing on an object. For the balloon to stay inflated, the pressure inside the balloon must be greater than atmospheric pressure. Additional pressure is necessary because the pressure inside the balloon must not only counter the atmospheric pressure but also hold the elastic rubber in the inflated position. If the mouth of the inflated balloon is opened (or the balloon pops), the extra air inside will quickly flow out because gases move from areas of high pressure to areas of lower pressure.

Part A of the activity shows that it is impossible to significantly inflate a balloon by mouth when the balloon is inside a bottle. The pressure of the air trapped inside the bottle prevents you from inflating the balloon. In order to blow up the balloon in the bottle, you not only need to blow enough air into the balloon to provide the pressure needed to stretch the rubber of the balloon, but you also have to apply enough pressure to compress the air trapped in the bottle. This compression is needed to make room for the inflated balloon. The activity shows this to be a real challenge. Even though gases are compressible, it is difficult for most of us to exert enough pressure just by blowing to compress the trapped air very much.

A balloon can be blown up in a bottle much more easily if there is an opening to allow air initially inside the bottle to escape to make room for the expanding balloon. If you seal the hole after inflating the balloon, the balloon will remain inflated even after you remove your mouth. For the balloon to deflate, it is necessary for air particles to occupy the volume previously occupied by the inflated balloon. However, the careful observer may notice that the bottom part of the plastic bottle slightly contracts around the inflated balloon or the balloon very slightly shrinks. The atmospheric pressure exerted on the open balloon is greater than the pressure in the region between the balloon and the bottle, which is enough to keep the balloon inflated except for this slight shrinkage. The balloon will deflate only when the hole in the side of the bottle is opened again so air can move into the bottle to replace the air coming out of the balloon.

Extensions 1 and 2 provide additional opportunities to observe the effects of air pressure. In Extension 1, squeezing the bottle forces some of the air from the bottle into the space occupied by the balloon. Because the balloon is mobile, this rush of air pushes the balloon through the neck of the bottle and, if the pressure is great enough, can even partially inflate the balloon inside out. In Extension 2,

Balloon in a Bottle

when the balloon is filled with water and the stopper removed, air moves into the bottle and forces the inflated balloon to contract. The water is propelled out of the balloon.

Assessment

Options:

- Have the students draw cartoons that illustrate this investigation.

- Have the students write three sentences telling what they learned in this activity.

- Have older students demonstrate the activity to younger students so that these younger students are able to show the activity to their parents and family.

- Have students brainstorm new and different activities they could do to demonstrate what they learned about air in this activity. Have the students present their demonstrations to the class.

Cross-Curricular Integration

Language arts:

- Have the students complete a science acrostic (acronym): Write the words "balloon" and "bottle" on the board. Instruct the students to choose one of these words and write it vertically on a piece of lined paper, with one letter to a line. Instruct the students to write one word, phrase, or sentence that begins with each letter of their word. Each word, phrase, or sentence must be related to the "Balloon in a Bottle" activity as in the following example:

    Big balloons can hold more air than little ones
    Air takes up space
    Latex is the stretchy stuff used to make balloons
    Lips make a seal
    Only one mouth per balloon, please
    Oh, I tried so hard to blow
    Now I know that balloons hold air

- Read aloud or suggest that students read *Wilbur's Space Machine,* by Lorna Balian (Humbug, ISBN 0-8234-0836-1), and discuss the science misconceptions in this story. Wilbur constructs a machine to manufacture "empty space" and contains the "empty space" in balloons. Unfortunately, there is soon no room left to live. So Wilbur ties the balloons to the house and it floats away. The book presents two science misconceptions. The balloons in the story would actually have been filled with air, not empty space. Also, balloons filled with room-temperature air don't float, so the house would not have floated away. The "Balloon in a Bottle" activity challenges the first misconception. To challenge the second misconception, blow up a balloon, tie it off, and release it.

Life science:

- Discuss why you should not blow up the same balloon someone else has blown up. (Compare to using the same silverware, combs, cups, etc.)

References

"The Bottled Balloon," *SuperScience*, October 1991, 28–29.

Ontario Science Center. *Scienceworks;* Addison-Wesley: Reading, MA, 1984; p 6.

Contributors

Mark Beck, Indian Meadows Primary School, Ft. Wayne, IN; Teaching Science with TOYS peer mentor.

Carol Schelbert, Randall School, Peru, IN; Teaching Science with TOYS, 1993–94.

Handout Masters

A master for the following handout is provided:

- The Air in There—Data Sheet

Copy as needed for classroom use.

Names _____   _____

_____   _____

Balloon in A Bottle
The Air in There—Data Sheet

Part A

1. Push a deflated balloon into the bottle without a hole and stretch the open end of the balloon back over the mouth of the bottle. (See figure.) Be sure you each have your OWN balloon. Predict what will happen when you blow into the balloon. _____

   _____

2. Now blow into your balloon. What happens? _____

   _____

3. Take your balloon out of the bottle and blow into it. What happens? _____

   _____

4. Can you explain the difference between what happened in Step 2 and Step 3? Discuss the results with your group. _____

   _____

   _____

Part B

5. Put your balloon in the bottle with the hole. Predict what will happen this time when you blow into the balloon. _____

   _____

6. Now blow into your balloon. What happens? Can you explain this? _____

   _____

   _____

7. What did you learn from this experiment? _____

   _____

   _____

Tissue in a Cup

Students investigate how to keep a tissue dry underwater.

sense of sight

Time Required

Setup   5 minutes
Performance   10–15 minutes
Cleanup   5 minutes

National Science Education Standards

Science as Inquiry Standards:

- Abilities Necessary to Do Scientific Inquiry

  Students use observations to construct a reasonable explanation
  for the tissue in the cup remaining dry when the cup is submerged
  and appeal to the evidence they obtained to support their
  explanation.

Physical Science Standards:

- Properties of Objects and Materials

  One of the three states of matter is the gas state. Students
  observe that the gases that make up air are not visible, yet they take
  up space.

A tissue in a cup

Materials

For Getting Ready
Per class
- nail or pushpin
- 2 clear, 10-ounce plastic cups made of soft plastic

*Don't use rigid plastic cups; they will crack when you try to make the holes. Solo® makes a
suitable cup with the letters PETE and recycling code 1 on the bottom of the cup.*

For the Procedure
Per class (works best as a demonstration)
- cup with hole prepared in Getting Ready
- 4 or 5 tissues
- (optional) tape
- food color
- paper towels
- 1 of the following large-mouthed containers (preferably clear):
  - small, plastic aquarium
  - plastic bucket
  - large beaker

A "pop-beaker" made from a cut-off 2-liter (L) bottle works well.

For Variations and Extensions

❶ ❷ ❹ All materials listed for the Procedure plus the following:
  • (optional) oil-based clay

❸ All materials listed for the Procedure plus the following:
  • different-shaped containers (such as a wide-mouthed cup, bowl, or plastic bag)
  • different cup materials (such as Styrofoam™, plastic, or cardboard)

Safety and Disposal

No special safety or disposal procedures are required.

Getting Ready

Push the nail or pushpin through the bottom of one of the flexible plastic cups to make a hole. (See Figure 1.) Remove the nail or pushpin. (The size of the hole will affect how quickly you see results in Step 7 of the Procedure. If you use a pushpin or small nail to make the holes, you will need to wait longer to see results than you would if you used a large nail.)

Figure 1: Push a nail through the bottom of a cup.

Introducing the Activity

Challenge the students to think of a method for keeping the inside bottom of an empty plastic cup dry while the cup is submerged in water. Give students an opportunity to brainstorm. Record all ideas. Tell students that you have a way to do this that you would like to show them.

Procedure

1. Crumple tissues and fit them tightly on the bottom of the plastic cup without the hole so that they won't fall out when the cup is turned upside down.
   You may need to use tape to hold the tissue in place.

2. With the cup upside down, push the cup down into a container of colored water until it is completely submerged. (See Figure 2.)

It is important to keep the cup very straight as you push.

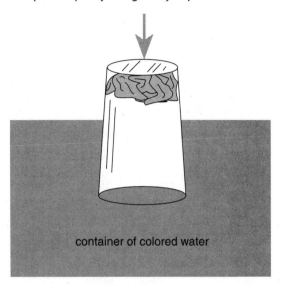

container of colored water

Figure 2: Push the cup underwater.

3. Withdraw the plastic cup from the water.

Remember to keep the cup very straight as you lift it.

4. Dry the lip and outside of the cup with a paper towel and remove the tissue from the cup.

5. Ask students, "What can you determine about the tissue by using your senses of touch and sight?" Have students record their observations.

6. Ask students to propose explanations for why the tissue is dry. Through class discussion, introduce the idea that air trapped in the cup kept the water out. Show students the cup with the hole in the bottom. Ask them to predict what will happen this time when you submerge the upside-down cup.

7. Repeat Steps 1–5 with the cup with the hole in the bottom. Have students record their observations.

If the hole in the cup is small, you may need to submerge it a while before something happens.

8. Dry the cup that has the hole in the bottom and crumple and insert a new tissue. Ask students to predict what will happen if you keep your finger over the hole and submerge the cup again. Repeat Steps 2–5 with your finger on the hole. Have students record their observations.

9. Have students share observations and discuss.

Variations and Extensions

1. Try using a cup with three holes punched in the bottom. Use tape or clay to seal the holes. When the cup is submerged, open all three holes. How quickly does the water fill the cup? Compare this with the cup that has only one hole. Students can predict which tissue will get wet first. Students can also estimate how many seconds it takes to get the tissue wet.

2. Repeat Extension 1 using single holes of different sizes.

3. Try this experiment using different-shaped containers (such as a wide-mouthed cup, bowl, plastic bag). Try different cup materials (such as Styrofoam, plastic, cardboard). Do the results change? Why or why not?

4. Set up the activity in a learning station and allow individual students to repeat the activity. Young students may need to use a clay ball to cover the hole.

5. Ask students to estimate and then test the number of tissues that can be put in the cup and successfully kept dry in this activity. (Pack them in tight!) Have the class create a histogram of the maximum number of tissues each group successfully kept dry.

Explanation

The following explanation is intended for the teacher's information. Modify the explanation for students as required.

Air is matter, and even though we can't see it, it takes up space. Air is trapped in the cup without a hole when you submerge it and in the cup with a hole when you seal the hole. The air in the cup keeps water out, so the tissues stay dry (unless the tissues should dislodge or slip downward). Some water will enter the open end of the cup because the air in the cup is slightly compressed as the cup is pushed into the water.

Repeating the Procedure with the cup with the open hole allows the air to be pushed out of the cup through the hole as water enters the cup. Since air can escape, water fills the cup, and the tissues become wet.

Assessment

Options:

*   Have students draw pictures of the investigation and describe it to someone, explaining why the tissue stayed dry in one case and not the other.

*   Ask students to choose one of the following objects: a clear plastic cup, a balloon, a paper lunch sack, or a small plastic bag. Ask, "What can you do with the object to show your learning buddy/friend/group that air takes up space?" Have the students demonstrate this principle with the object they have chosen.

- Tell students to imagine that a friend said that a cup that looks empty has nothing inside it. Do they agree or disagree? How could they respond to show their friend their ideas about what is in the cup?

Cross-Curricular Integration

Language arts:
- Make a class book about air. Have each student draw a picture about what the student has learned about air or something he or she likes to do with air and write sentences to tell about the picture.
- Have students read the nonfiction book, *The Science Book of Air,* by Neil Ardley (Harcourt Brace Jovanovich, ISBN 0-15-200578-1). This book contains simple experiments demonstrating basic principles of air and flight. Cooperative learning groups could choose activities to demonstrate to the class.

Life science:
- Discuss how diving spiders carry air with them underwater.

Social studies:
- Ask students to describe the types of activities that people might do underwater that would require them to take air with them. *Scuba diving, riding in a submarine.*
- Research the history and use of diving bells. (The original diving bells were hollow structures open at one end that were lowered into the ocean much like the cup in this activity.)

Reference

Kaskel, A. *Principles of Science: Activity-Centered Program Teacher's Guide;* Charles E. Merrill: Columbus, OH; pp 29–30.

Contributors

Lynda Dunlap, Southwestern Elementary School, Patriot, OH; Teaching Science with TOYS, 1991.
Susy Hasecoster, Liberty Elementary School, Liberty, IN; Teaching Science with TOYS, 1991.
Diana James, Farmers Elementary School, Farmers, KY; Teaching Science with TOYS, 1991.
Carole Pope, Southwestern Elementary School, Patriot, OH; Teaching Science with TOYS, 1991.
Jackie Toombs, Norwood Middle School, Norwood, OH; Teaching Science with TOYS, 1992–93.
Ann Veith, Rosedale Elementary School, Middletown, OH; Teaching Science with TOYS, 1991–92.

sense of hearing

Big Ben

Paper Cup Telephone

Big Ben

Students make a noise amplifier and discover how sound travels through solids.

Big Ben toy

Time Required

Setup	5 minutes
Performance	20 minutes
Cleanup	5 minutes

National Science Education Standards

Science as Inquiry Standards:

- Abilities Necessary to Do Scientific Inquiry

  Students conduct a simple investigation in which they use their sense of hearing to observe the movement of sound through air and solids and make systematic observations of each.

Physical Science Standards:

- Properties of Objects and Materials

  An observable property of some materials is the sound they produce when hit or banged.

- Position and Motion of Objects

  Sound is produced by vibrating objects. The sound waves produced by vibrating objects can move through both gases and solids. When sound moves through gases, much of it is dissipated before reaching the ear. When sound moves directly to the ear through solids (such as paper cups and string), much more reaches the ear.

Materials

For the Procedure
Per student
- 2, 3-foot pieces of string or yarn
- metal coat hanger
- 2 buttons or 2 paper clips
- 2, 4-ounce paper cups
- sharpened pencil

For the Extensions
❶ All materials listed for the Procedure plus the following:
- various metal objects, such as a spoon, fork, metal ring from a ring stand, piece of heavy copper wire, or aluminum foil folded in a triangle

Safety and Disposal

Remind students to be careful not to hit other students when they're swinging the toys. No special disposal procedures are required.

Introducing the Activity

Explain to the students that sound waves are invisible but are all around us. Sound waves in the air occur when an object vibrates. When the waves reach the ear, we hear the sound.

Have students tap on a table and listen closely. Then have them put an ear to the table and repeat the tapping. Discuss which tapping sounds louder.

Procedure

Part A: Make the Toy

Have each student construct a Big Ben toy as follows:

1. Use a sharpened pencil to poke a hole in the bottom of one paper cup and thread one end of a string through this hole.

2. Tie a button or paper clip to the end of the string in the cup and pull the string projecting out the bottom of the cup so that the button or paper clip is firmly against the inside bottom of the cup. (See Figure 1.)

Figure 1: Tie a button to the end of the string and pull it back into the cup.

3. Tie the end of the string projecting from the base of the cup to one end of the hanger as shown in Figure 2.

4. Repeat Steps 1–3 for a second cup and string.

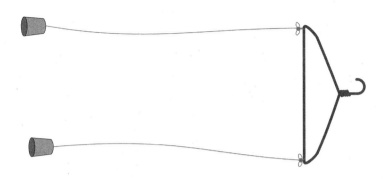

Figure 2: Assemble a Big Ben toy as shown.

Part B: Explore Sound with the Toy

1. Have students hold one cup in each hand. (The hanger will swing in front of them.) They should NOT hold the cups to their ears yet.

2. Have each student swing the hanger gently so that it hits a desk or wall. Observe the sound produced. Emphasize that the sound waves traveled through the air and reached the ears, allowing the students to hear the sound.

3. Now tell the students to hold the cups up to their ears and swing the hanger so that it hits the same object as in Step 2. Have them observe the sound produced. Emphasize that the sound waves that reach the ear now traveled up the string into the ears. Ask, "How is this sound different from the sound produced when the cups were not held to your ears?" *The sound is louder, or amplified.* (The reason that the sound is louder is that the waves traveled through the string, a solid, rather than through the air, a gas.)

4. Instruct the students to observe differences in the sounds produced as they hold the cups to their ears and strike their hangers against different surfaces.

Extensions

1. Vary the sound by using different metal objects (such as spoons, forks, a metal ring from a ring stand, a piece of heavy copper wire, or aluminum foil folded in a triangle) in place of the hanger.

2. Have students do the "Hear, Hear!" Take-Home Activity (provided) outside of school with an adult partner.

Explanation

> *The following explanation is intended for the teacher's information. Modify the explanation for students as required.*

In this activity, sound is produced when the hanger is hit against various objects. The vibration produced by the collision creates sound waves which eventually reach your ear. This sound energy is eventually passed to tiny bones in our ears, causing the bones to vibrate. When these bones vibrate, our brains give us the message that we hear a sound. The more energy that reaches the ear, the louder we perceive the sound to be.

When the sound energy from the hanger travels through the air to your ear, the sound is relatively soft. This is because the only route the sound energy from the hanger has to get to your ear is through the air. In this process, the energy must be transferred from the coat hanger to gas particles in the air. These fast-moving particles transfer this energy via collisions with other gas particles. The energy quickly dissipates around the room, with only a small amount reaching our ears.

When the Big Ben toy is used to carry the sound energy to your ears, the sound is much louder. This happens because the string provides an alternative and more effective path for the energy to travel. Because the particles in the string are much closer together than the particles in the air, the energy from the hanger can pass directly to our ears. Less energy dissipates to other areas of the room.

In Step 4, students observe differences in the sounds produced when the hanger hits different objects. The properties of the various materials students hit with the hanger will affect the vibration produced by the collision and thus the sound heard through the cups.

Cross-Curricular Integration

Life science:
- Have students study the parts of the ear to learn how humans and other animals hear. What adaptations do different animals have to enhance their hearing ability?

Music:
- Have students study how different musical instruments produce sound.

References

Hewitt, P.G. *Conceptual Physics,* 7th ed.; HarperCollins: Glenview, IL, 1993.
Kirkpatrick, L.D.; Wheeler, G.F. *Physics: A World View;* Saunders College: Philadelphia, PA, 1992.

Contributors

Phyllis Wilkes, Harvey Rice School, Cleveland, OH; Teaching Science with TOYS, 1991–92.
Linda See, Wildwood School, Middletown, OH; Teaching Science with TOYS Teacher/
    Administrator Program, 1994–95.

Handout Master

A master for the following handout is provided:
- Hear, Hear!—Take-Home Activity

Copy as needed for classroom use.

Big Ben

Hear, Hear!—Take-Home Activity

Date _____

Dear Adult Partner(s):

We have been studying the sense of hearing. We have studied diagrams of the ear and learned that sound waves travel through the air and through solids. Today we did an investigation called "Big Ben." We threaded a piece of string through a hole in the bottom of a paper cup. We tied a paper clip or button to the end of the string in the cup and pulled the end of the string projecting out the bottom of the cup so that the button or paper clip was firmly lodged against the inside bottom of the cup. We then tied the free end of the string to one side of a coat hanger and repeated the process with a second cup and string. We used this toy to study sound by swinging the hanger gently so that it struck various objects. First we held the cups in front of us and struck the hanger against an object. Then we put the cups over our ears and struck the hanger again. We tried striking the hanger against several objects and comparing sounds.

Please try the investigation yourself and see if you can figure out why the activity is called "Big Ben." Then ask your child to explain how the toy works. (Note: The energy produced by the hanger striking objects normally is transferred to gas particles in the air and dissipates quickly around the room. Only a small portion of that energy reaches our ears. The string provides a more effective path for the energy to travel. When we place the cups over our ears, the energy from the hanger can pass through the string directly to our ears, and the sound we hear is therefore louder.)

The following are further investigations you can try:

• Hit the hanger against a variety of objects. Are the sounds different?
• Bend the hanger and hit it against objects. Are the sounds different?
• Cover the hanger with yarn or cloth and hit it against objects. Are the sounds different?

Discuss the results with your child. Have fun!

Sincerely,

_____

Paper Cup Telephone

Students use the fact that sound travels through solids to build a functional Paper Cup Telephone.

Paper Cup Telephone apparatus

Time Required

Setup	10 minutes
Performance	30 minutes
Cleanup	5 minutes

National Science Education Standards

Science as Inquiry Standards:

- Abilities Necessary to Do Scientific Inquiry

    Students conduct a simple investigation in which they use their sense of hearing to observe the movement of sound through solids (the strings and cups of Paper Cup Telephones) and make systematic observations.

Physical Science Standards:

- Position and Motion of Objects

    Sound is produced by vibrating objects. The sound waves produced by vibrating objects can move through solids and be transmitted in several directions simultaneously through connected materials such as the Paper Cup Telephone party lines.

Materials

For Introducing the Activity
- (optional) rubber band or all of the following: salt, a balloon, and a clean, empty tin can (such as a soup can)

For the Procedure
Per pair of students

- 2 paper or foam cups

Paper cups are more effective since the cup bottom is a separate piece, and its vibration is not dampened by the students' hands on the sides of the cup.

- 12-foot length of fishing line or string
- 2 plastic buttons or paper clips
- sharpened pencil (if holes are not punched in Getting Ready)

For Variations and Extensions
❶ All materials for the Procedure plus the following:
- strings with different thicknesses

❷ Per student
- Paper Cup Telephones
- juice can telephone made from the following:
  ○ paper clip
  ○ 4- to 6-foot piece of fishing line or strong string
  ○ frozen concentrated juice can

➤ *Cans with aluminum bases work better than those with steel bases because aluminum vibrates more readily.*

  ○ plastic button
  ○ hammer
  ○ screwdriver or nail

➤ *The hammer and screwdriver or nail, intended for teacher use only, are needed to make juice can telephones the first time Extension 2 is done.*

Safety and Disposal

You may want to have students put their names on their cup phones and use only their own phones to avoid spreading germs in the class. Have students carefully look where they're going, as the taut strings of the telephones can be difficult to see. No special disposal procedures are required.

Getting Ready

1. (optional) Punch holes in the bottoms of the paper cups (or see Part A, Step 1 of the Procedure).

2. For Extension 2, puncture the metal ends of the juice cans with a hammer and a screwdriver or nail, using the hammer to drive the sharper end of the screwdriver or nail through the metal. Thread the string through this hole and anchor with a plastic button on the inside of the can.

Introducing the Activity

Options:

- Begin the activity with a demonstration and discussion of what a vibration is. A vibration can be demonstrated either by 1) having students pluck a stretched rubber band and observe the wave motion and the sound that results; or 2) putting salt on a balloon that is stretched over the top of a soup can (much like skin is stretched to form an eardrum), clapping your hands in front of the can, and having students watch the salt crystals jump.

- Have students knock on their desks and listen to the sound. Then have them put their ears to the desks' surfaces and knock on their desks again. This activity shows that sound waves travel through air and through solids, too.

Procedure

Part A: Making the Telephones

Have each pair of students perform Steps 1–4:

1. Use a sharpened pencil to poke a hole in the bottom of each of the two cups.

2. Feed one end of a 12-foot length of string through the bottom of one cup.

3. Anchor the string in the cup by tying a button or paper clip onto the end of the string and pulling it tight back into the cup. (See Figure 1.)

4. Repeat Steps 2 and 3 with the other cup and the other end of the string.

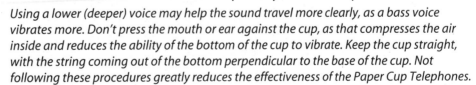

Figure 1: Tie a button to the end of the string and pull it back into the cup.

Part B: Using the Telephones

Warn students to be careful moving around the classroom during this part of the Procedure, as the taut strings of the telephones can be difficult to see.

1. Have each pair spread out so that the string is extended between the cups.

2. Have each student hold his or her cup securely with both hands.

Keep the string pulled tight and not touching anything else. No fingers should be touching the bottom of the cup or the string.

3. One person should talk softly into the cup while the other holds his or her cup to the ear to listen. Talk into the cup clearly and distinctly.

Using a lower (deeper) voice may help the sound travel more clearly, as a bass voice vibrates more. Don't press the mouth or ear against the cup, as that compresses the air inside and reduces the ability of the bottom of the cup to vibrate. Keep the cup straight, with the string coming out of the bottom perpendicular to the base of the cup. Not following these procedures greatly reduces the effectiveness of the Paper Cup Telephones.

4. Have pairs team up so that every four students has a set of phones. Have one of the pairs of students temporarily store their phones by winding the string around one cup and placing this cup inside the other.

5. Have one student in each team talk into the phone while a second listens, as in Step 3. The other two students should stand alongside the stretched string and observe. Ask, "Can you see any movement in the string?" (Students will

probably not be able to see the string vibrating.) Let the observing students use one finger to gently touch the string. (They should be able to feel the vibration.) Ask the listening student how touching the string affected the sound heard.

6. Have students get out the second set of phones and make a party line by wrapping one pair's string around the center of another pair's string, as shown in Figure 2. Pull all of the strings tight as before. One person should talk while the others listen.

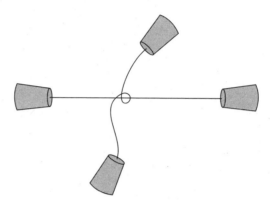

Figure 2: Make a party line by wrapping one pair's string around the center of another pair's string.

7. Wrap another pair's string to the party line to have six-way calling. One person should talk while the others listen.

8. Ask students what they learned about the movement of sound through solids. Have students explain and give evidence for their answers.

Variations and Extensions

1. Use different thicknesses of string between the paper cups. Test to see which thickness produces the clearest sounds. (Thinner strings should produce stronger vibration, and thus the clearest sounds.)

2. Give each student a partially assembled juice can telephone (prepared in Getting Ready) and have them complete the assembly as follows: Make a hook from a paper clip as shown in Figure 3. Tie the free end of the string to one end of the paper clip. Have one pair of students stretch taut their Paper Cup Telephone set made in the Procedure. These students are on the main line. Have the other students hook their juice can telephones to the main line using the paper clip hooks. Remind the students to keep their lines stretched tight for the best vibration transmission. Have each student take a turn speaking into his or her can. All students should hear the messages.

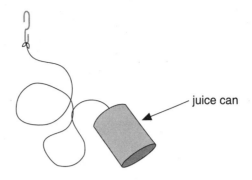

juice can

Figure 3: Make a hook from a paper clip and tie it to the free end of the string.

Explanation

 The following explanation is intended for the teacher's information. Modify the explanation for students as required.

In the activity students find that sound is transmitted through solids, such as string, cup, juice can, and paper clips. The particles that make up a solid are touching. This allows them to easily transmit sound energy from one particle to another. The sound travels in waves along the string of the Paper Cup Telephone. These waves cause the taut string to vibrate. (See Big Ben for a more detailed explanation.)

Cross-Curricular Integration

Life science:
- Have students study the parts of the mouth and throat that make it possible for humans to speak. How are vibrations created as we speak?
- Have students research whales to learn about the sounds they make and how sound travels through water.

Music:
- Have students study how musical instruments produce sound.

Social studies:
- Research the development of the telephone and find out how telephones transmit sound.

References

Hewitt, P.G. *Conceptual Physics;* Addison-Wesley: Reading, MA, 1987; pp 369–372.
"Make Your Own Phone," *Super Science Red.* January 1990, supplement.

Contributors

Ann Veith (activity developer), Rosedale Elementary School, Middletown, OH; Teaching Science with TOYS, 1992–93.

Paula Matre, Heritage Hill Elementary School, Cincinnati, OH; Teaching Science with TOYS, 1993.

Janice McPherson, Kings Mills Elementary School, Kings Mills, OH; Teaching Science with TOYS, 1993.

sense of smell

Identifying Substances by Smell
Smelly Balloons
The Scratch-and-Sniff Challenge

Identifying Substances by Smell

Students learn about the sense of smell while identifying substances by their scents.

. . . .
Time Required

Setup	15	minutes the first time the activity is done; 10 minutes thereafter
Performance	15–30	minutes
Cleanup	5	minutes

National Science Education Standards

Science as Inquiry Standards:

- Abilities Necessary to Do Scientific Inquiry

  Students conduct a simple investigation in which they use their sense of smell to examine smelly substances and make systematic observations.

  Students communicate the results of their investigation by sharing observations and discussion as a class.

Physical Science Standards:

- Properties of Objects and Materials

  An observable property of some materials is smell.

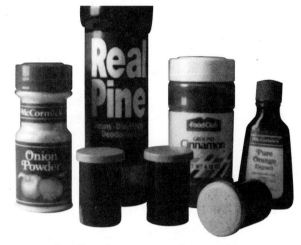

Smelly substances and containers

. . . .

Materials

For Getting Ready
Per class
- several film canisters or other small, opaque containers with plastic lids
- extra plastic lid for each container
- cotton balls
- pushpin
- several scents or smelly substances such as the following:

 Use liquid or powdered substances that will be easy to pour into small containers.

- ○ banana
- ○ chocolate
- ○ cinnamon
- ○ coconut
- ○ lemon
- ○ mint
- ○ onion
- ○ orange
- ○ pine (such as pine-scented cleaner)
- ○ strawberry

For the Procedure
Per class
- numbered scent containers prepared in Getting Ready

For Variations and Extensions
❶ Per class
- concentrated scent
- facial tissue

Safety and Disposal

Take care that younger children do not drink or splash flavorings into their faces. Warn students about the dangers of smelling substances that they do not know for sure are safe, or anything that is labeled "Use in a well-ventilated area" or "Do not inhale vapor." No special disposal procedures are required.

Getting Ready

1. Place a cotton ball into each container that will hold a liquid sample.

2. Prepare a lid with a hole for each container by poking several holes in the plastic lid with a pushpin.

3. Pour a small amount of each scent into a container. (Pour liquid samples onto cotton balls.) Place a lid without holes on each container. Number each container and keep a key so that you can later reveal the identity of the scents. (Be sure to put the numbers on the containers and not on the lids.)

Introducing the Activity

Discuss smells that students like or dislike, and have the students describe them. Ask students how they know which ingredients are on their favorite pizza without looking or tasting.

When introducing any activity that involves the smelling of potentially unknown odors, instruct the students about protecting themselves. Show the students how to use the wafting procedure and remind them to avoid prolonged inhalation of objectionable odors. (See Figure 1.) Such odors are typically not good for us.

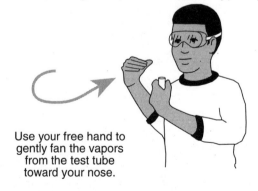

Use your free hand to gently fan the vapors from the test tube toward your nose.

Figure 1: Show your students how to use the wafting procedure to smell unknown odors.

Procedure

1. Write a list of all the scents you will be using on the board. Have students copy this list to make their own data sheets, listing the scents in one column and leaving a space beside each scent name to record the number of the container they think contains that scent.

2. Remove the lids without holes from the containers and replace them with lids with holes.

3. Pass the numbered containers around the room. Instruct the students not to open the containers, but to attempt to identify the odor by first wafting the odors from holes in the top of each container. If an odor is not detected, the container can be waved closer to the nose.

4. Have students attempt to match the number of each container with the appropriate scent on the data sheet.

5. When all students have had a chance to smell each container, have them discuss their findings as a class. Which smells were easy to identify? Which smells were difficult to identify? Why?

6. Reveal which smells were in which containers. If there are discrepancies between student guesses and scents used, discuss why students may have misidentified the smells. (Students may be unfamiliar with that smell; the smell may be in the same family as something else; the student may have a cold or otherwise be unable to smell clearly; etc.)

Variations and Extensions

1. Introduce scents one at a time to the entire class by pouring some concentrate onto a facial tissue and waving the tissue around. Have the students raise their hands as the odor reaches them, but tell them not to say the name out loud.

2. Ask the students to list situations when their sense of smell
   a. provides pleasure,
   b. is useful,
   c. warns of danger, and
   d. causes displeasure.

3. Have students do the "Smells Around the House" Take-Home Activity (provided) outside of school with an adult partner.

Explanation

 The following explanation is intended for the teacher's information. Modify the explanation for students as required.

The flavor extracts used in this activity are concentrates of the more dilute naturally occurring flavors. Imitation extracts can also be used; these are synthetic replicas of the naturally occurring compounds. The extracts and other smelly substances used in the activity contain very tiny particles that are so small that under normal circumstances they cannot be seen. You can, however, detect their presence by smelling them. The particles of the extracts or other smelly substances typically reach the nose by first evaporating (changing from a liquid to a gas) or subliming (changing from a solid to a gas). Once in the gaseous state, the particles travel through the air until they reach the nose. There they set off a complex series of chemical reactions in the body that allows the person to detect their odor. (Tiny particles of liquids and solids can also travel through the air as aerosols and similarly trigger the chemical sequence in the nose to allow the person to sense the odor.)

Our noses are very sensitive to smells. When we have a head cold, we are reminded of how much we depend on our sense of smell. Since our senses of smell and taste are closely related, when smell is not working properly, neither is taste. Besides allowing us to enjoy things that smell good, our sense of smell can also warn us of danger such as spoiled food or smoke.

Cross-Curricular Integration

Language arts:
- Have students select a smell that brings back memories and write a story about those memories.
- Have students write descriptive paragraphs that paint pictures of places by describing smells. Examples include the county fair, a summer garden, or their grandparents' house at a favorite holiday time.
- Have students write about the Take-Home Activity in which students identify different smells around the house. (See the "Smells Around the House" Take-Home Activity.)

Life science:
- Discuss situations in which smelling things might be dangerous. If the label says "Use in a well-ventilated area" or "Do not inhale vapor," the substance would be dangerous to smell.
- Study different organisms' abilities to detect odors. How are these adaptations valuable to them?

Math:
- Create bar graphs showing the number of students who identified each smell correctly.

Social studies:
- The smells of foods from less familiar cultures may be difficult for students to identify. Have students cook and smell unfamiliar foods from different countries (for example, curry/India, chili/Mexico, and fish sauce/Vietnam).
- Have students list products that are valuable because of the way they smell.
- Ask students to research careers that require the use of our sense of smell.

Reference

Woodward, L. *Experimental Chemistry Kit Activities for Elementary Grades* (unpublished); University of Southwestern Louisiana: Lafayette, LA, 1987.

Contributors

Mary Hurst, McKinley Elementary School, Middletown, OH; Teaching Science with TOYS, 1994.

Tom Pierson, Edgewood Middle School, Hamilton, OH; Teaching Science with TOYS, 1994.

Handout Masters

A master for the following handout is provided:

• Smells Around the House—Take-Home Activity

Copy as needed for classroom use.

Identifying Substances by Smell
Smells Around the House—Take-Home Activity

Date _____

Dear Adult Partner(s):

We have been trying to identify smells in science class. Please help us add to our list by helping your child write a list of items around the house that can be identified by smell. Be sure to caution your child that some items are dangerous to smell because they give off poisonous or burning fumes. Beware of substances whose labels say "Use in a well-ventilated area" or "Do not inhale fumes (vapors)."

I hope you enjoy doing this activity with your child.

Sincerely,

_____

Reproduced from *Exploring Matter with **TOYS**,* published by McGraw-Hill.

Smelly Balloons

Students discover that scents can travel through the wall of a balloon.

Time Required

Setup	5–15 minutes
Performance	15–25 minutes
Cleanup	5 minutes

National Science Education Standards

Science as Inquiry Standards:

* Abilities Necessary to Do Scientific Inquiry

   Students conduct a simple investigation in which they use their sense of smell to examine smelly substances placed inside balloons and make systematic observations.

Physical Science Standards:

* Properties of Objects and Materials

   An observable property of some materials is smell.

   One of the three states of matter is the gas state. Particles of smelly materials used in this activity move through the wall of a latex balloon, evaporate, and move through the air until they reach special receptors inside our noses.

A balloon with extract and a dropper

Materials

For Introducing the Activity
* various scents such as peanut butter, lemon, roses, popcorn, and coffee

For the Procedure
Per group
* dropper
* latex balloon
* flavoring extract such as vanilla, peppermint, or orange

Each group should use a different extract and a different-colored balloon.

* crayons or colored markers corresponding to the balloon colors
* (optional) glue

For Variations and Extensions
❶ Per class
* natural and artificial flavorings

141

❷ Per class
  • assorted spices or vegetables with strong odors such as cloves, nutmeg, garlic, and onions
  • latex balloon for each spice or vegetable
  • marker

❸ All materials listed for the Procedure plus the following:
  • Mylar, other metallized, or plastic-treated balloons
  • access to a freezer

❹ All materials listed for the Procedure except
  • substitute zipper-type plastic bags for balloons

Safety and Disposal

You should blow up the balloons for very young students. There is a danger that they might inhale instead of blow and get the balloon stuck in the windpipe. No special disposal procedures are required.

Getting Ready

For younger students, you may wish to do Step 2 of the Procedure in advance.

Introducing the Activity

When introducing any activity that involves the smelling of potentially unknown odors, instruct the students about protecting themselves. Show the students how to use the wafting procedure and remind them to avoid prolonged inhalation of objectionable odors. (See Figure 1.) Such odors are typically not good for us. Tell students that in this activity they will be asked to identify the contents of a balloon by smell alone. Emphasize that in spite of the fact that you have selected safe materials for the activity, they should use the wafting procedure as a first line of detection, smelling the balloon more closely only after they have established it is not an offensive odor.

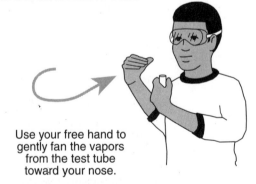

Use your free hand to gently fan the vapors from the test tube toward your nose.

Figure 1: Show your students how to use the wafting procedure to smell unknown odors.

In addition to discussing the wafting procedure, you may wish to do one or more of the following introductory activities.

Options:

- Introduce the activity with a discussion about using our sense of smell to make observations.

- The week before you do this activity, feature a different smell each day (such as peanut butter, lemon, roses, popcorn, and coffee). Have the room smell like these substances when the students enter in the morning. Discuss the odors smelled, and talk about how those odors reach our noses and are detected. Responses to this topic can lead into a discussion on air. Blow up a balloon and seal it. Discuss that the balloon is filled with air. Leave the balloon for a week and have the students observe that it decreases in size. Ask students what they observe about the balloon and how the air got out of the balloon. Have the students put part of their shirts over their mouths and blow through them. Although the students can't see the pores in the material, they should observe that air passes through the material. Relate this to the deflating balloon. Even though the students can't see the pores in the balloon, they should understand that the pores are there.

- For the upper grades, discuss how the particles responsible for odors travel based upon particle theory.

Procedure

1. Have the students color the balloons on the "What's the Scent?" Data Sheet (provided) to correspond with the balloons to be used and write the color names next to the balloons.

2. Instruct each group to put one or two drops of their extract into their balloon by inserting a dropper as far as possible into the balloon. This way the extract does not get on the neck of the balloon.

 Students must avoid getting extract on their hands. It will interfere with their handling and smelling the balloons. Students should also avoid letting other groups see the extract they're using. Younger students need to be shown how to insert the dropper deeply enough in the balloon to avoid getting extract around the lip of the balloon.

3. Have a member of each group blow up the group's balloon, tie it off, and shake it a few times.

4. Have groups pass the balloons around. Smell them, first using the wafting procedure and then smelling more closely. Record the odors they think they can detect.

5. Have the students indicate their guesses by cutting out the circles on the "Scent Circles" Template (provided) and gluing them to the Data Sheet or by writing the names of the scents on the Data Sheet.

 If you want students to use Scent Circles and if you use different extracts than those included in the template, draw your own scent pictures in the blank circles provided.

6. After all the groups are finished making observations, make a list of the odors students identified for each balloon, and then have each "home group" tell what was actually used in their balloon.

Variations and Extensions

1. Compare artificial and natural extracts (for example, artificial vanilla versus natural vanilla). Can students detect a difference?

2. Compare extracts to fragrant spices or vegetables (such as nutmeg, cloves, or chopped garlic or onion). Place dry spices in balloons to determine if their odor travels through the balloon wall.

3. Place extract in a balloon as described in the Procedure and find out how long your students can detect the odor. Have them smell the balloon every hour or so and record observations. Repeat this variation using a Mylar, other metallized, or plastic-treated balloon. Compare the permeability of the different balloon materials.

4. Substitute zipper-type plastic bags for the balloons. Have students compare the time it takes to smell extracts through balloons (fast), room-temperature plastic bags (slow), and plastic bags from the freezer (very slow).

5. Make up several pairs of balloons with various extracts and challenge the students to use their sense of smell to find both balloons of each pair. (Each balloon in a pair should contain the same extract.)

6. Have students do the "How Do Smells Travel?" Take-Home Activity (provided) at home with an adult partner.

Explanation

The following explanation is intended for the teacher's information. Modify the explanation for students as required.

All matter is made up of tiny particles. They are so small that under normal conditions you can't see them, but in some cases you can detect their presence by smelling them. The extracts and other smelly substances used in this activity contain particles that have certain characteristic odors. When these smelly particles reach special receptors inside our noses, a series of complex chemical reactions begins that ultimately results in the perception that you smell a particular substance.

This activity shows that the particles responsible for certain odors can pass through the wall of a common latex rubber balloon. Leading students to this conclusion should be the goal of this activity for teachers of lower grades. The following discussion is provided for teachers and/or for students in the upper grades.

To explain the idea that the particles responsible for the odor of the extract can pass through the balloon, we need to consider three important factors: the volatility of the particles responsible for odors, the permeability of balloons to these particles, and the solubility of one chemical in another.

Flavoring extracts are usually a mixture of several components that have been extracted from a seed, flower, or plant using alcohol or water. The molecules that are responsible for the characteristic odor of the extract are usually fairly volatile, which means they easily vaporize from the liquid to the gaseous state.

If you have ever observed an air- or helium-filled latex balloon over a period of days, you have seen the balloon shrink as the gaseous molecules inside moved to the outside through the microscopic pores in the balloon. The speed at which a gas diffuses is related to its molecular mass. The larger the molecular mass, the slower the gas diffuses. That's why helium-filled balloons shrink faster than air-filled balloons. (Helium atoms have less mass than the nitrogen molecules and oxygen molecules found in air.)

While it is possible that some molecules of the extract pass through the pores in the balloon, it is important to note that these molecules of extract are considerably larger and more massive than molecules of water or alcohol that are typically the solvents for the extracts. Vanillin, for example, is the molecule in vanilla that gives it its characteristic odor. Vanillin has the chemical formula $C_8H_8O_3$. On a per molecule basis, vanillin is about 38 times more massive than helium, 18 times more massive than water, and about five times more massive than nitrogen or oxygen gas. Because the odor of vanillin is detected outside the balloon very quickly, this would lead us to conclude that another factor must be involved in the movement of the odor molecules through the balloon walls.

What then, could this other factor be? It is proposed that the molecules of extract actually interact with and perhaps even dissolve in the latex layer of the balloon. On a molecular level, the latex layer is actually relatively thick, containing several layers of long, interwoven latex molecules. Molecules of extract may gradually dissolve in the strands of latex as they move through the latex. When the extract reaches the outside of the balloon, it evaporates to the gaseous state and moves through the air to our noses.

Assessment

The ability of gas to pass through porous materials can be demonstrated through a whole group exercise. The goal of the following whole-group assessment activity is to enable students to experience the activity and be able to state what is happening in their own words.

1. Take the class to a large area such as a gymnasium.

2. Instruct a majority of the class to form a circle, holding hands, legs spread apart so their feet are touching their neighbors' feet. Explain to the class that these students represent the balloon. Have a few students go to the middle of the circle to represent the particles responsible for the scent. (See Figure 2.)

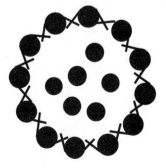

Figure 2: Students form a circular "balloon" with "scent" particles in the middle.

3. Direct the students in the middle to demonstrate how, as scent particles, they might get through a porous material like the balloon. Students will then generate ideas about being able to slowly crawl under or step over the linked arms and legs of the people in the circle, or loosen and move through the linked arms and legs. Discuss the speed at which the students should leave the middle of the circle. Was the odor detected immediately? Did the odor all leave at once, or did some continue to stay in the balloon?

4. Next ask the "balloon" students what they could do to represent a nonporous material. The class could then provide ideas about dropping their arms, bringing their legs together, and standing shoulder to shoulder. The circle is obviously smaller, but it becomes quite evident that the students that represent the particles responsible for the scent now do not have an easy way out of the "balloon" unless it is broken.

5. (optional) Provide an assessment activity to determine individual understanding. Students can describe in writing or draw a picture of what took place in the gym and/or what they believed happened with the particles responsible for the scent inside the balloon.

Cross-Curricular Integration

Art:
• Have students make craft items that have a smell, such as potpourri.

Language arts:
Have students do one of the following writing exercises:
• Write questions relating to the activity for their classmates to answer. The questions should concentrate on "who," "what," "why," "where," "when," and "how."
• Write an "Interview with a Nose" as a summary for the activity. The interview questions should be based on the activity, and the nose's answers should explain what happened in the activity.

Life science:
Have students find answers for one or more of the following questions:
• How do the human senses work?
• How do animals use pheromones to communicate?
• What kinds of animals (for example, some types of nocturnal animals) use smell as their predominant sense?

Reference

Mebane, R.C.; Rybolt, T.R. *Adventures with Atoms and Molecules;* Enslow: Hillside, NJ, 1985; pp 8–9.

Contributors

Susan Brutsche, Bellevue City Schools, Bellevue, OH; Teaching Science with TOYS, 1991–92.

Donna Essman, Stanton Primary School, New Boston, OH; Teaching Science with TOYS, 1991–92.

Marilyn Hayes, John XXIII Elementary School, Middletown, OH; Teaching Science with TOYS, 1990–91.

Bonnie Marx, Miami East Junior High School, Piqua, OH; Teaching Science with TOYS, 1991–92.

Jill Swango, Brownsburg Junior High School, Brownsburg, IN; Teaching Science with TOYS, 1992–93.

James Warren, New Boston Elementary School, New Boston, OH; Teaching Science with TOYS, 1991–92.

Handout Masters

Masters for the following handouts are provided:

- What's the Scent?—Data Sheet
- Scent Circles—Template
- How Do Smells Travel?—Take-Home Activity

Copy as needed for classroom use.

Name _____   Date _____

Smelly Balloons
What's the Scent?—Data Sheet

Write the balloon colors and color the balloons in the first column. Record your scent guesses in the second column and the actual scents in the third column.

Color of Balloon	Guesses	Actual Scent

Smelly Balloons
Scent Circles—Template

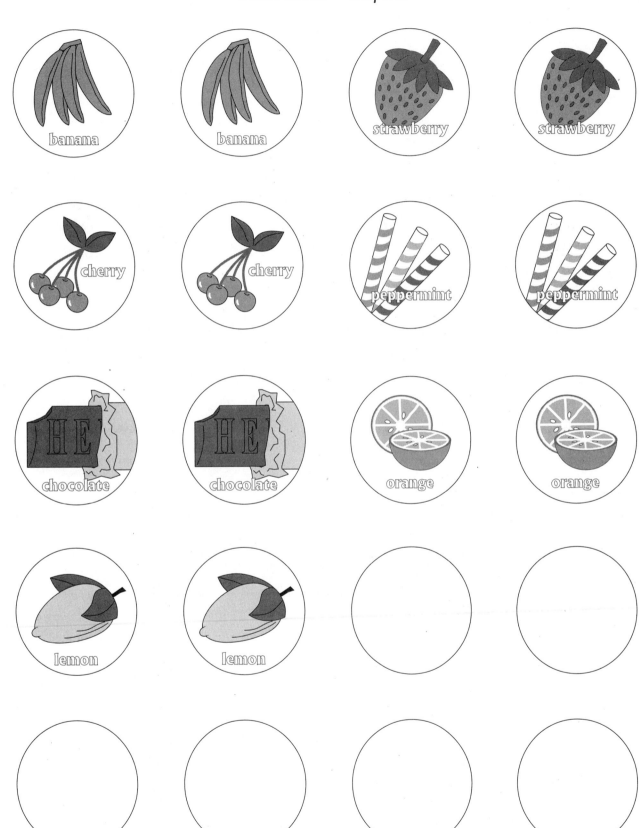

Reproduced from *Exploring Matter with* **TOYS**, published by McGraw-Hill.

149

Smelly Balloons
How Do Smells Travel?—Take-Home Activity

Date:_____

Dear:_____

Today I learned something at school using my ⟨ NOSE ⟩

We learned that my nose is used for one of my five senses. We put different smells (scents) into colored balloons. The scent my group used was _____. Our group had to guess what scent was used in the other balloons by smelling the outside of each balloon. We learned that a balloon is porous. That means the smell can pass through it.

We can do a similar activity at home. (Pick one.)

❶ Put some drops of a natural or artificial extract inside a balloon. (Be careful not to get any on your hands or on the outside of the balloon.) Blow up the balloon and tie it shut, then have _____ guess what we put inside.

❷ Do Activity 1, but instead of using an extract, use a solid with a strong odor, such as cloves or garlic.

❸ An easier way to explain the process of a scent passing through a porous material would be to stand behind a window with a screen. Keep the window closed. Waft a strong smelling substance past the window while others on the other side of the window and screen try to smell it. Can they smell it? Why or why not? Now open that same window and waft the substance past the screen. Can they smell the scent this time? Why or why not? What prevented the scent from passing to the person on the other side of the window and screen? What was the porous material in this experiment?

Sincerely,

Name of student: _____

Adult Partner(s): Please feel free to make comments to the teacher on the back of this page.

Reproduced from *Exploring Matter with* **TOYS**, published by McGraw-Hill.

The Scratch-and-Sniff Challenge

Students identify substances by smell and investigate how microencapsulation works.

Time Required

Setup	10–20 minutes
Performance	30–40 minutes
Cleanup	5 minutes

National Science Education Standards

Science as Inquiry Standards:

- Abilities Necessary to Do Scientific Inquiry

  Students conduct a simple investigation in which they release smelly substances from baggies and scratch-and-sniff stickers and use their sense of smell to make systematic observations.

  Students communicate the results of their investigation by sharing observations. These are recorded on an observation sheet for discussion.

Physical Science Standards:

- Properties of Objects and Materials

  An observable property of some materials is smell. When these materials are encapsulated or encased, their odors are often less apparent. Breaking or otherwise opening the container releases the material so its smell is more easily detected.

Scratch-and-sniff stickers

Materials

For Getting Ready
Per class
- permanent marker

Per group
- cotton ball, cotton makeup removal pad, or small piece of felt or sponge
- small zipper-type plastic bag
- 1 of the following "smelly" substances:

vanilla	almond	smoke (liquid)
coconut	peanut butter	banana
mint	grape	pineapple
lemon	strawberry	Vick's® vapor rub
orange	chocolate	Kool-Aid®
cinnamon	pine (cleaner)	Jell-O®

  ➤ *Use a different smelly substance for each group.*

For Introducing the Activity
Per class
• several scratch-and-sniff stickers

For the Procedure
Part A, per group
• smelly bag prepared in Getting Ready

Part B, per pair of students
• scratch-and-sniff sticker
• small paper bag

For Variations and Extensions
❶ Per class
• smelly bags used in Part A of the Procedure

❷ Per class
• sheet of large bubble wrap
• syringe with small needle

The syringe is for teacher use only. Syringes with needles are available from Flinn Scientific, 800/452-1261 (# AP1149) and from Frey Scientific, 800/225-FREY (3cc syringe, # F04060). Syringes might also be available from a veterinarian or a farm supply store.

• transparent tape or hot-melt glue stick (can be melted with either a hot-melt glue gun or candle and matches)

Safety and Disposal

If Variation 2 is done, inject flavored extracts into the bubble wrap ahead of time. Be careful not to stick yourself with the needle. Keep the needle covered with the plastic tip except when filling the needle or injecting the extracts. Students should NEVER have access to the syringe. Store the syringe safely for future use. The teacher should be the only one to use the glue gun.

Getting Ready

1. If smelly solid substances are used, dissolve them in small amounts of water to make concentrated solutions.

2. Prepare a smelly bag for each group by moistening a cotton ball, pad, or piece of felt with two or three drops of a different smelly solution and placing it into a small zipper-type plastic bag. Using a permanent marker, number each bag. Record the number and contents of each bag for your reference. You need to prepare only one bag of each smell to be tested. Before using with the class, blow a little air into each bag to simulate an encapsulated bubble on a scratch-and-sniff sticker.

Introducing the Activity

Show the students some scratch-and-sniff stickers. Pass one or two around the class and allow the students to scratch, sniff, and identify the odors. Challenge the class to suggest explanations for how the scratch-and-sniff sticker is made, why it must be scratched to let the smell out, and how the smell gets from the sticker to a person's nose. Let them brainstorm ideas in groups and document their ideas in pictures or notes.

When introducing any activity that involves the smelling of potentially unknown odors, instruct the students about protecting themselves. Show the students how to use the wafting procedure and remind them to avoid prolonged inhalation of objectionable odors. (See Figure 1.) Such odors are typically not good for us.

Use your free hand to gently fan the vapors from the test tube toward your nose.

Figure 1: Show your students how to use the wafting procedure to smell unknown odors.

Procedure

Part A: The Smelly Bags

1. Divide students into groups and distribute one smelly bag and a "Guess that Smell!" Observation Sheet (provided) to each group.

2. Ask the members of each group to smell their smelly bag by opening the bag and wafting the odor toward their noses without removing the cotton, felt, or sponge from the bag.

3. The group members should discuss what they believe the smell to be and record their guess by the appropriate number on the Observation Sheet.

4. Once each group has had a chance to record their guess, have someone in each group blow a little air into the bag (without letting his or her mouth touch the bag) in order to re-inflate the "encapsulated bubble," reseal the bag, and pass it on to another group. The groups should then repeat Steps 2 and 3 for each bag.

5. Once all the smelly bags have been tested by each group, compare the class results for each bag. Discuss why groups might have indicated different identifications, and then compare the class results to your answer key. Each group should color in the stars next to their correct guesses on the Observation Sheet.

Part B: The Sniff Challenge

Because most scratch-and-sniff stickers are shaped like the object they are supposed to smell like, have students scratch and sniff the stickers inside the bags to avoid recognizing the smells by the appearance of the stickers.

1. Have students work in pairs and give each pair a scratch-and-sniff sticker inside a small paper bag.

2. Have each member of the pair reach into the bag and scratch and sniff the sticker and guess what the odor is without talking to the other. Once both students have made their own guesses, have the pair discuss what they believe the odor is.

3. Have the pairs report their findings and compare their results to what the package claims the odor is. Class discussion should focus not only on the identification of the smells, but also on why the stickers needed to be scratched to release the odor, how the stickers are made, and how the odor gets from the sticker to their noses. Challenge students to draw a picture of how they think the scratch-and-sniff sticker would look if it were magnified. Compare these drawings with the ideas proposed before the activity.

Variations and Extensions

1. As an alternative to Part A of the Procedure, place the smelly bags on a bookshelf or long table. Have each student write his or her name on a sheet of paper and number a line for each smelly bag. Write all the odors the students will smell on the board. Divide the class into pairs. (The activity works well if each team is composed of a stronger learner and a more needy learner.) Have students smell the bags and record their guesses of the identities of the odors. After all teams have smelled all the bags, compare their guesses to your identification key and record the number of correct answers for each smell on a graph. Use the graph to extract math information such as: How many students correctly identified coconut? How many students correctly identified vanilla? Is the number of students correctly identifying coconut greater than or less than the number of students correctly identifying vanilla? End the session with a discussion of why some smells might be more easily identified than others.

Be certain to inject the extracts ahead of time. Students should NEVER have access to the syringe. Be careful not to stick yourself. Keep the needle covered with the plastic tip except when filling the needle or injecting the extracts. Store the syringe safely for future use.

2. Use sheets of plastic bubble wrap to simulate the microencapsulation of smelly substances in scratch-and-sniff stickers: Inject flavored extracts into the bubble through the back of the sheet using a hypodermic syringe. (See Figure 2.) Seal the hole with transparent tape or hot-melt glue soon after the injection is made. (A candle can be used to melt the glue if a glue gun is not available.) Prepared bubbles can last several days if they are well sealed. During the activity, have students pop the bubbles as they would when they usually play with bubble wrap. This extension closely simulates what happens when the students scratch and pop the tiny capsules on the stickers.

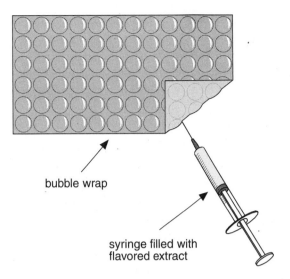

bubble wrap

syringe filled with
flavored extract

Figure 2: Inject flavored extracts into bubble wrap.

Explanation

 The following explanation is intended for the teacher's information. Modify the explanation for students as required.

All matter is made up of tiny particles. They are so small that under normal conditions they can't be seen. However, in some cases you can detect the presence of the particles by smelling them. Each of the extracts and other smelly substances used in this activity contains particles that have characteristic odors. When these smelly particles reach special receptors on the inside of our noses, a series of complex chemical reactions begins that ultimately results in the perception that you smell a particular substance.

When the smelly substances are encapsulated in the scratch-and-sniff stickers or the plastic bags, the smelly particles are for the most part sealed in. However, once the sticker is scratched so that some of the encapsulated bubbles pop or the bag is opened, some of the smelly particles evaporate (change from the liquid to the gaseous state). The gas particles quickly diffuse (spread out) through the air until some reach our noses.

Assessment

- Have students draw pictures or act out the process of a "smell" getting to the nose. If doing an enactment, have several students surround another to "encapsulate" the "smell." Place a "nose" some distance away from the encapsulated sample. Break the "capsule." Have the "smell" travel to the "nose."

- Have students write or tell stories as if they were scent particles and describe their trips to noses. You can determine the level of students' understanding by reading their stories.

Cross-Curricular Integration

Home, safety, and career:
- Because sniffing glue and organic solvents continues to be a problem with dangerous consequences, you may wish to lead the class in a discussion of the dangers associated with such practices.

Language arts:
- Have students make scratch-and-sniff books using commercially available stickers.
- Have students write stories or poems about smells that make them remember things that have happened to them.
- Have students write or tell stories about a detective trying to find the source of a strange scent. These stories could be illustrated by gluing extract-soaked cotton balls at appropriate places in the stories.
- Read aloud or suggest that students read one or more of the following books:
  - *Noses Are for Smelling Roses,* by Eve Morel (Grosset & Dunlap, ISBN 0-448-02808-5)
    By scratching and smelling pages, the reader shares some fragrances as a mother and her two children go through an ordinary day's activities.
  - *A Sniff in Time,* by Susan Saunders (Atheneum, ISBN 0-689-30890-6)
    One day in James' life is much like the next until a hungry wizard drops by for dinner and leaves James with the unsettling ability to smell into the future.
  - *Sweet as a Rose,* by Albert Carr and Lawrence Lowery (Holt, Rinehart, & Winston, ISBN 0-03081170-8)
    A young child walks throughout his town and describes various smells he experiences. The reader can guess what the items are from clues provided.
  - *The Gingerbread Man* (any version)
    A gingerbread man smells very good when he is baking. He runs away from everyone who wants to eat him.

Life science:
- Demonstrate how the senses can work together by holding a tasting party. Have students taste the same foods while holding their noses and then not holding their noses.
- Study how a scent travels to the nose, how it is subsequently transmitted to the brain, and how the brain determines what the scent is. Hide one scent in the room and have students act as detectives to find the scent. Then hide three scents in the room to demonstrate that after a period of time it is difficult to separate the different scents.
- Study the role of pheromones in animal communication.

Math:
- Have students measure and graph how long the smell from each sticker lasts in the room.
- Have students walk toward the source of a scent and record the distance from which it is first detected.

Reference

Schultz, E. "Pop and Sniff Experimentation: A High-Sensory-Impact Teaching Device," *Journal of Chemical Education.* 1987, 64(9), 797–798.

Contributors

Theresa Applegate, Lincoln Heights Elementary School, Cincinnati, OH; Teaching Science with TOYS, 1993–94.

Opal Chambers, Taft Elementary School, Middletown, OH; Teaching Science with TOYS, 1990–91.

Cherie Kuhn, Tri-County North Elementary School, Lewisburg, OH; Teaching Science with TOYS, 1992.

Jean McCormack, Liberty Elementary School, Liberty, IN; Teaching Science with TOYS, 1991–92.

Diane Pieratt, Tri-County North Elementary School, Lewisburg, OH; Teaching Science with TOYS, 1992.

Handout Master

A master for the following handout is provided:

• Guess that Smell!—Observation Sheet

Copy as needed for classroom use.

Names _____   _____

_____   _____

The Scratch-and-Sniff Challenge
Guess that Smell!—Observation Sheet

Record your guesses next to each number.

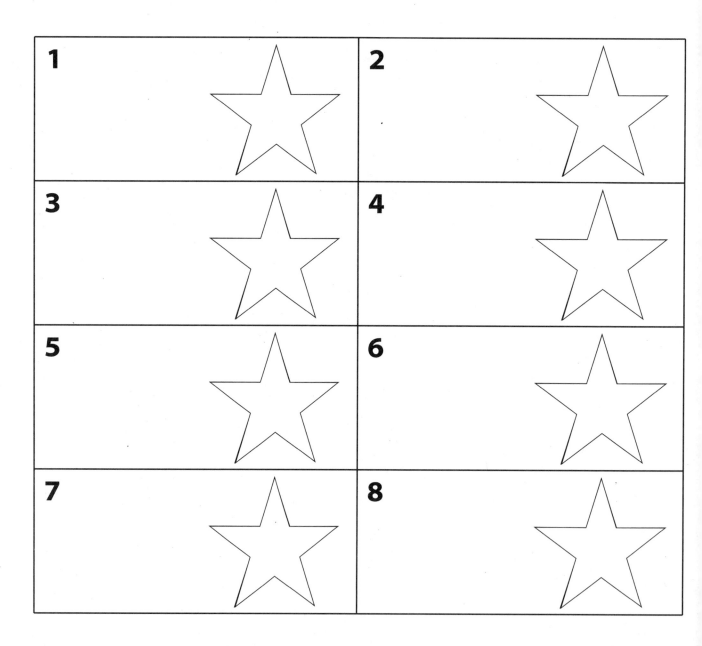

If your guess was correct, color the star in that box.

Reproduced from *Exploring Matter with TOYS*, published by McGraw-Hill.

sense of taste

Jumbled-Up Jello

Using Taste to Solve a Mystery

Food that Pops

Jumbled-Up Jello

Students conclude that the sense of sight can fool us (things are not always what they appear to be) and that our sense of taste is a more reliable predictor for this activity.

Time Required

Setup	45 minutes
	+ 3 hours for the gelatin to set
Performance	15 minutes
Cleanup	10 minutes

National Science Education Standards

Science as Inquiry Standards:

• Abilities Necessary to Do Scientific Inquiry

Students conduct a simple investigation in which they attempt to first identify gelatin flavors based on sight alone and then based on sight and taste. In the activity, the information provided by color is inconsistent with the students' expectations for the taste, making accurate prediction based on sight alone extremely unlikely.

Students use observations of color to propose flavors for the gelatin cubes and appeal to the evidence they obtained to support their ideas.

Flavoring, food color, and gelatin

Physical Science Standards:

• Properties of Objects and Materials

Color and taste are both observable properties of a material.

Materials

For Getting Ready

Per class
• materials to make 2 wrapped packages:
  ◦ two boxes
  ◦ newspaper
  ◦ wrapping paper
  ◦ an item students would consider nice or an inexpensive treat for each student (such as a sticker or a party favor)
  ◦ an item or collection of items students would consider unpleasant (such as rocks or dirt)
  ◦ decorative bow
  ◦ tape

- materials to make gelatin cubes:
  - 2 envelopes of unflavored gelatin
  - ½ cup sugar
  - water
  - 2, 8-inch by 8-inch baking pans
  - 2 bowls
  - stirring spoon
  - measuring cup and measuring spoons
  - red and blue food colors
  - strawberry and lemon flavorings
  - saucepan
  - hot plate

For Introducing the Activity
Per class
- 2 wrapped packages prepared in Getting Ready

For the Procedure
Per class
- gelatin cubes prepared in Getting Ready
- napkins
- (optional) paper plates

For the Variation
Per class
- 2 light-colored flavors of Kool-Aid®

 Light-colored Kool-Aid is most effective for this variation because the original color can be easily masked by the food color without creating an unappealing muddy color.

- 2 food colors that are different and darker than the Kool-Aid colors
- pitcher
- spoon
- disposable cups

Safety and Disposal

Remind students that they should not taste unknown substances unless a trusted adult such as a teacher or parent assures them that it is safe to do so. No special procedures are required for disposal.

Getting Ready

For Introducing the Activity, put an item the students would consider "nice" (or special inexpensive "treats" for students, such as stickers or party favors) in a box and wrap it sloppily with newspaper. Put an item or collection of items students would consider unappealing (such as rocks or dirt) in another box and wrap it attractively with wrapping paper and a bow.

The day before class, prepare the gelatin cubes for the Procedure according to the following recipes:

Purple Gelatin Cubes
1 envelope unflavored gelatin
¼ cup (60 mL) sugar
5 teaspoons (25 mL) cold water
1 teaspoon (5 mL) strawberry flavoring
⅝ cup (150 mL) boiling water
4 drops blue food color

Red Gelatin Cubes
1 envelope unflavored gelatin
¼ cup (60 mL) sugar
5 teaspoons (25 mL) cold water
1 teaspoon (5 mL) lemon flavoring
⅝ cup (150 mL) boiling water
4 drops red food color

Follow this recipe for each batch:
Heat 1¼ cups water to boiling in a saucepan on a hot plate. (This is enough water for both batches.) For each batch, mix the food color, cold water, and flavoring together in a bowl. Sprinkle the gelatin over the mixture. Let stand for 1 minute. Add ⅝ cup boiling water and stir until gelatin is completely dissolved. Pour into an 8-inch by 8-inch baking pan. Chill until firm (about 3 hours). Cut into small pieces so that you have one piece of each batch for each student.

Introducing the Activity

Ask students if they can always tell everything they need to know about something just by using their sense of sight. Show the students the two wrapped packages. Ask them which one their sense of sight would have them choose. Have two volunteers unwrap the boxes and display the contents. Have the students discuss the fact that the appearance didn't reflect the contents of the boxes. Explain to the class that they are going to do an investigation that may require more than their sense of sight to identify the substance.

Procedure

1. Ask the students to use their sense of sight to predict the flavor of each gelatin cube and to record those predictions on their "Tricky Taste Test" Data Sheets (provided). Have students share the reasons for their predictions. (Students' experiences with foods will have led them to form various color-flavor associations.)

2. Instruct the students to taste the cubes and name the flavors they detect on their Data Sheet.

3. Compare the flavors students predicted using the sense of sight to the flavors named using the sense of taste.

4. Reveal the actual identity of each flavor.

5. Have students record the actual flavors on the Data Sheet. Did their predictions using sight match the actual flavors? Were they more successful using a combination of sight and taste? Discuss the fact that often we cannot rely totally on one sense to give us accurate and complete information.

Variation

Make two different flavors of Kool-Aid and color each with a food color that is different than the original color. Have students predict flavors using the sense of sight and then try to identify the flavors using the sense of taste. Discuss as in Steps 3–5 of the Procedure.

Explanation

The following explanation is intended for the teacher's information. Modify the explanation for students as required.

We rarely use only one of the five senses at a time. Instead, we use a combination of senses in order to accurately gather information about an object. In this activity, students predict tastes based on appearances. Since the students have learned to associate tastes with colors, they probably expected the red gelatin to taste like strawberries or cherries and the purple gelatin to taste like grapes.

As much as we associate one sensory impression with another, however, we cannot replace one sense with another. As students found out in this investigation, seeing does not necessarily give the whole picture. Instead, it often takes a combination of the five senses to gather complete information about an object. In this activity, students use the senses of taste and smell to help them formulate a more complete picture of what the flavors actually are.

Cross-Curricular Integration

Language arts:
- Have students write about an experience of their own in which they discovered that something was not exactly what it seemed. For example, perhaps a neighbor who looked grumpy turned out to be kind, a new food that didn't look appetizing tasted delicious, a book with a dull cover was very exciting to read, or a brand-new bike had wheels that wouldn't turn.
- Read aloud or suggest that students read one or more of the following books:
  - *Tasting,* by Kathie B. Smith and Victoria Crenson (Troll, ISBN 0-8167-1015-5)
    Uses a question-and-answer format to explain our sense of taste.
  - *A Tasting Party,* by Jane Belk Moncure (Childrens Press, ISBN 0-516-43253-2)
    Flowers, leaves, seeds, roots, fruits, dairy foods, and meats are sampled at different types of food-tasting parties.
  - *Green Eggs and Ham,* by Dr. Seuss (Beginner, ISBN 0-394-80016-8)
    "Things are not always what they might appear to be" is the message cooked up in this creative tale by Dr. Suess. The story unfolds in classic cumulative rhyme as Sam I Am tries to share his Green Eggs and Ham with an unwilling acquaintance.

Life science:
- Discuss nutrition. Have students split into groups of two to tell each other about a food they disliked because of its appearance but found they liked once they tasted it.

Social studies:

- Have a class discussion relating to times in history when groups of people have been stereotyped and discriminated against because of their appearance. Read *Marian Anderson,* by Anne Tedards (Chelsea House, ISBN 07910-0216-0). This book tells the story of a distinguished opera and concert singer who was denied the right to sing inside the Capitol Building in Washington, D.C., because she was black. Discuss how prejudice can deny people the opportunity to use their individual talents.

Contributors

Peggy Kulczewski, Lincoln Elementary School, Monmouth, IL; Teaching Science with TOYS, 1994.
Cindy Waltershausen, Western Illinois University, Macomb, IL; Teaching Science with TOYS, 1994.

Handout Master

A master for the following student handout is provided:
- Tricky Taste Test—Data Sheet

Copy as needed for classroom use.

Name _____

Date _____

Jumbled-Up Jello
Tricky Taste Test—Data Sheet

Color in the blocks.	Predict the flavor using sight only.	Give a reason for your prediction.	Name the flavor you taste.	Write the actual flavor.
Red				
Purple				

Using Taste to Solve a Mystery

Students use four of the five senses but rely most heavily on taste to identify four white solids.

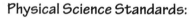

Time Required

Setup   10–20 minutes
Performance   20 minutes
Cleanup   15 minutes

National Science Education Standards

Science as Inquiry Standards:

- Abilities Necessary to Do Scientific Inquiry

    Students conduct a simple investigation in which they examine four white solids and make systematic observations.

    Students use observations to propose identities for the four solids and appeal to the evidence they obtained to support their ideas.

    Students communicate the results of their investigation by sharing observations and discussing as a class.

Physical Science Standards:

- Properties of Objects and Materials

    The white solids can be described by their properties, and those properties can be used to sort and identify the solids.

Four white solids—salt, flour, corn starch, and sugar

Materials

For Getting Ready
Per class
- popcorn
- masking tape and pen for labels
- salt
- sugar (granulated or powdered)
- corn starch
- flour
- 4 plain, uniform containers

Per student
- 2 zipper-type plastic bags

For Introducing the Activity
Per student
- small bag (approximately ¼ cup) of salted popcorn
- small bag (approximately ¼ cup) of unsalted popcorn

For the Procedure
Per class
- box or bag of each of the following white solids in their original containers:
  - salt
  - sugar (granulated or powdered)
  - flour
  - corn starch
- 4 white solids in unmarked, uniform containers prepared in Getting Ready
- ½ teaspoon measuring spoon

Per student
- light-colored crayon
- black (or dark) construction paper
- slice of bread
- napkins
- 2 plastic bags

For Variations and Extensions
❷ All of the materials listed for the Procedure, except
- substitute powdered sugar for corn starch

❸ Per student
- 4 cups
- salt
- sugar
- corn starch
- flour

❹ All of the materials listed for the Procedure, plus the following:
- water
- 4 cups
- stirrer

Safety and Disposal

Emphasize to students that not all white solids are edible. Caution the students not to eat an unknown substance unless an adult in charge gives permission, and assure the students that the four white powders used in this activity are edible. No special disposal procedures are required.

Getting Ready

1. Make a small bag of unsalted popcorn for each student. Label these bags "A."

2. Make a small bag of salted popcorn for each student. Label these bags "B."

3. Put some of the salt, sugar, corn starch and flour into plain, uniform containers. (Put enough of the solids in the unmarked containers so that each student can measure ¼ teaspoon of each solid in the Procedure.) Label the containers 1–4 and keep a record for yourself that shows which substance is in which container.

4. For younger students, do Steps 2–4 of the Procedure. Put each measured quantity into a labeled plastic bag.

Introducing the Activity

Options:

- To make sure students can recognize the taste of salt, give each student a small bag of unsalted popcorn marked "A." Allow the students to eat the popcorn. Have students use all their senses to observe the "A" popcorn. Have them brainstorm words that describe the popcorn. Write these words on the board. Then give each student a bag of salted (no butter) popcorn marked "B." Have students use all their senses to observe the "B" popcorn. Allow students to eat the popcorn. Have students use all their senses to observe the "B" popcorn. Have them brainstorm words that describe the popcorn. Write these words on the board. The words should be very similar, except the word "salty." Make sure all of the students recognize the taste of salt.

- Allow students to examine known samples of salt, sugar, flour, and corn starch several days or more in advance of this activity. This will provide a basis for the identification done in this activity.

Procedure

Show the students the original containers of salt, sugar, corn starch, and flour. Tell them they will receive a small sample of each of these solids but not be told which is which. It will be up to them to identify the solids. Because these are common solid food items, the students will be allowed to taste these unknowns as long as they follow good health rules.

Have each student complete Steps 1–9, then do Steps 10 and 11 as a class.

1. Wash and dry your hands.

2. Fold a sheet of black (or dark) construction paper horizontally and vertically to divide the paper into four equal sections and use a light-colored crayon to trace the fold lines.

3. Number the four sections 1–4 with a light-colored crayon.

4. Measure ½ teaspoon of each substance and place it on the appropriate section. (Place the substance from container 1 in block 1; container 2 to block 2; container 3 to block 3; and container 4 to block 4.)

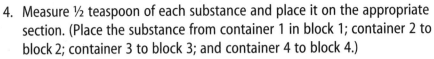

You may wish to do Steps 2–4 for younger students.

5. Use every sense except taste to observe the unknown substances and write your observations on the "What Is It?" Data Sheet (provided).

6. Taste one of the substances by wetting your finger with saliva and placing it on the solid. Then, touch the finger to your tongue. Record your observations based on taste.

7. Cleanse your palate by blotting your tongue with a piece of bread. (The bread helps dry the tongue and remove the taste of the previous substance.) Place the used bread on a napkin.

8. Repeat Steps 6 and 7 with the remaining substances.

9. Use the observations collected in the previous steps to propose an identity for each of the four white solids.

10. Ask students to share their ideas about the identities of the solids. Encourage students to present evidence for their ideas based on their observations.

11. Reveal the identities of the solids. Since students may not be familiar with some of the solids, discuss the uses of each solid in baking or cooking. Ask, "Can you think of any non-food, non-cooking uses for these solids?" (Salt can be used to melt ice in the winter, corn starch can be used as baby powder or in Corn Starch Putty, and flour and salt can be used to make homemade clay.) Have students finish answering the questions on the Data Sheet.

Variations and Extensions

1. For younger students, you may wish to substitute powdered sugar for corn starch. (While powdered sugar is a mixture of ground-up sugar and cornstarch, the sweetness of it should make it an easily identifiable solid.)

2. Have older students test the four substances to see which of them dissolve in water. Have students observe the consistency of the liquids. Can they identify the substances based on this characteristic and their senses of sight and touch?

3. Have students do the "What Do We Eat?" Take-Home Activity (provided) outside of school with an adult partner.

Explanation

The following explanation is intended for the teacher's information. Modify the explanation for students as required.

In this activity students use all five senses to help them identify four "unknown" solids. The students would have difficulty identifying the solids without the sense of taste, as most students have little direct experience using these solids. Upon tasting, students can typically identify salt, granular sugar, and powdered sugar (used in Variation 1). Flour and corn starch are much more difficult for younger students to identify.

Most children have more sensitive taste buds than adults. After tasting each ingredient, the taste buds must be cleaned of the "taste of the substance" to reduce interferences between samples. This is usually done by eating a small piece of bread or rinsing with water.

Assessment

Use the "How Did You Solve the Mystery?" Assessment Sheet (provided) as a guide or checklist for the individual groups of students. Circulate through the room while they work and ask them to tell you their answers for the first four questions. Ask an additional question or two from the remaining questions and have the students answer orally. Conclude with a group discussion, allowing students to share their observations and results. Guide the students to summarize what they learned from the experiment.

Cross-Curricular Integration

Language arts:
- Have students write about the dangers of tasting unknown substances.
- Read aloud or suggest that students read one or more of the following books:
  - *Beginning to Learn About Tasting*, by Richard Allington (Raintree, ISBN 0-817-2129-22)
    Introduces the four basic tastes (sweet, sour, bitter, and salty) along with 15 other types of tastes and textures such as spicy and crunchy. Recipes and activities are included.
  - *Tasting Things*, by Allan Fowler (Childrens Press, ISBN 0-516-4947-16)
    A simple introduction to the sense of taste.
  - *Touch, Taste, and Smell*, by Steve Parker (Franklin Watts, ISBN 0-531-2460-78)
    Examines the senses of touch, taste, and smell, and the bodily processes contributing to them.

Life science:
- Draw a map of the tongue. Mark the areas of the tongue which taste the salt and sugar.
- Have students study the food pyramid and the relative importance of sugar, salt, flour, and corn starch in the diet. Discuss how these substances fit into a healthy diet.

Social studies:
- Discuss why companies that create blends of tea or coffee, make wine, or manufacture chocolate might employ people to work as tasters.

Contributors

Marla Creamer, Tecumseh Elementary School, Xenia, OH; Teaching Science with TOYS, 1994.

Rita Glavan, St. Pius X Elementary School, Reynoldsburg, OH; Teaching Science with TOYS, 1994.

Jeanne Tuschl, Tulip Grove Elementary School, Hermitage, TN; Teaching Science with TOYS, 1994.

Handout Masters

Masters for the following handouts are provided:

* What Is It?—Data Sheet
* What Do We Eat?—Take-Home Activity
* How Did You Solve the Mystery?—Assessment Sheet

Copy as needed for classroom use.

Name _____

Date _____

Using Taste to Solve a Mystery

What Is It?—Data Sheet

Write your observations of each numbered substance in the boxes.

What is it?

	1	2	3	4
How does it look?				
How does it feel?				
How does it smell?				
How does it taste?				
What do you think it is? Why?				
What is it?				

Using Taste to Solve a Mystery

What Do We Eat?—Take-Home Activity

Date _____

Dear Adult Partner(s):

In science class today, we observed and identified salt, sugar, corn starch, and flour. Your child can describe our investigation to you. With your help, the students will continue to develop their science skills at home! Please help them to complete the Food Chart and answer the question. Have your child write down the name of some foods he or she ate. For each food, have your child put an X in the appropriate box or boxes to show whether that food had salt, sugar, flour, or corn starch as an ingredient. (A food may contain more than one of these substances.) You might encourage your child to look at the ingredients listed on packages or to ask about the ingredients you use in the dishes you prepare. This will help your child to confirm his or her observations. Thank you for your assistance with this assignment.

Sincerely,

_____

Food Chart				
Name of the food I ate	**Salt**	**Sugar**	**Corn starch**	**Flour**

How could you tell the foods contained these substances?

_____

_____

_____

Name _____   Date _____

Using Taste to Solve a Mystery
How Did You Solve the Mystery?—Assessment Sheet

1. Write each container number next to the substance it contains.

   sugar _____   flour _____   corn starch _____   salt _____

2. What properties were the same for the white solids? _____

   _____

   _____

3. What properties were different for the white solids? _____

   _____

   _____

4. What senses gave you the most help in identifying the white solids?_____

   _____

   _____

5. Which taste was the easiest to detect?_____

   _____

   _____

6. What foods do you eat that taste salty? _____

   _____

7. What foods do you eat that taste sweet? _____

   _____

Food that Pops

Students use their senses to explore foods that pop.

Time Required

Setup	10 minutes
Performance	30–45 minutes
Cleanup	10 minutes

National Science Education Standards

Science as Inquiry Standards:

- Abilities Necessary to Do Scientific Inquiry

  Students conduct a simple investigation in which they compare several foods that fizz and pop and make systematic observations.

  Students communicate the results of their investigation by sharing observations.

Physical Science Standards:

- Properties of Objects and Materials

  One of the properties of the active ingredients in Zotz® candies is the ability to react with each other to produce a new substance.

  The three states of matter are solid, liquid, and gas. The ingredients of Zotz candies are solids. When some of those ingredients react with liquid water (from saliva), a gas (carbon dioxide) is produced. Pop Rocks™ are solids with carbon dioxide gas bubbles trapped inside. When the solid is dissolved by a liquid (saliva), the trapped gas is released.

Zotz, a popping candy

Materials

For the Procedure
Part A, per student

- 1 Zotz

If Zotz candies are unavailable at a grocery store, you may find them at a bulk candy or novelty food store.

- package of Pop Rocks

Pop Rocks are available from Toys R Us stores.

- several sheets of paper towels or paper plates
- small cup of water
- dropper
- magnifying lens

For Variations and Extensions

❷ Per class
- Zotz
- package of Alka-Seltzer®
- 2 small, clear plastic cups

Safety and Disposal

Stress the importance of never placing materials in the mouth or tasting things during science activities unless specifically directed by the teacher to do so. No special disposal procedures are required.

Procedure

Part A: Zotz Pops

1. Pass out one Zotz candy in its wrapper to each student, and tell them to unwrap the Zotz, look at them, smell them, and put them in their mouths WITHOUT biting them. Read the label to the class.

2. Allow the students to suck on the candies for a short time and describe their observations. *The candy is sweet and fruit-flavored.*

3. Have the students continue sucking on their candies until they observe something new. Have students raise their hands when they observe this change.

4. Crack open an unused Zotz to show what it looks like inside. Pass it around for students to observe the dry, white powdery substance in the middle.

5. Place this powder on the overhead and spread it out in a thin layer. Add one or two drops of water to the powder to show the students what happened inside their mouths.

6. Challenge the students to describe what they see and relate that to what happened within their mouths. Tell students that the fizzing is the result of a chemical change.

Part B: Pop Rocks Challenge

 Have each student complete a "Pop Rocks Challenge" Observation Sheet (provided) while doing this investigation.

1. Have each group open a Pop Rocks package and place a few Pop Rocks on a paper towel.

2. After observing Pop Rocks, have groups use droppers to place drops of water on some of the Pop Rocks and observe changes with magnifying lenses.

3. Have students place dry Pop Rocks in their mouths. Remind them not to swallow until the pieces have completely dissolved. Have students "listen and feel" their observations.

4. Discuss what happened and why. Tell students that the popping is the result of a physical change.

5. Ask students whether they think holding the candy in their hands would make it pop.

6. Have students hold a large Pop Rock or several small pieces in their hands, close their hands, and bring their hands near their ears to listen. What happens? *They pop!*

7. Discuss student observations. Ask, "Do you think this physical change was caused by moisture or body heat or both? How could we find out?" Discuss students' ideas and try some if appropriate.

Variations and Extensions

1. Read the labels of Zotz and Pop Rocks and relate the ingredients to the reasons for the pop in each case.

2. Compare the reaction of Alka-Seltzer in water and the inside of the Zotz in water. Read the labels and discuss similarities and differences of the reactions and the contents.

Explanation

 The following explanation is intended for the teacher's information. Modify the explanation for students as required.

The active ingredients in Zotz are sodium bicarbonate, tartaric acid, and citric acid in the dry form. Sodium bicarbonate is baking soda. Citric acid is found in citrus fruits. Tartaric acid is found in many fruits; cream of tartar, derived from the fermentation of wine, is a potassium salt of tartaric acid. When these ingredients are combined with water, a chemical reaction that produces carbon dioxide gas takes place.

The popping sensation observed in the activity resulted when the sodium bicarbonate reacted with these two acids to form carbon dioxide bubbles, which break on the tongue. However, the reaction did not occur until water (or saliva) was added. The water dissolved the solids and allowed them to react with one another to form this new product.

Reading the label of Pop Rocks reveals that the candy does not contain sodium bicarbonate or either of the acids found in the Zotz. Rather, the pop that results is caused by the release of carbon dioxide bubbles that are encapsulated within the candy. Addition of water weakens the structure of the solid, allowing the gas to break through and cause the pop. This is a physical change, rather than a chemical reaction, because no new products are produced. Pop Rocks, Cosmic Candy, and similar carbonated sweets are typically made as a mixture of crystalline sugars, corn syrup, dextrin, flavorings, and water. The mixture is heated until the sugar dissolves. The water is then evaporated using a vacuum pump to form a viscous sugar mixture. At this point, carbon dioxide gas is pumped into the mixture at pressures between 34–51 atmospheres (atm). (There is 1 atm pressure at sea level.) The hot mixture is held below 138°C and stirred for several minutes. This process, developed by scientists at General Foods Corporation, forces bubbles into the candy mixture. The carbonate mixture is allowed to cool while still under pressure, which traps the carbon dioxide gas in the solid candy.

Cross-Curricular Integration

Music:
- As a class, write a song about Pop Rocks or Zotz to the tune of "Pop Goes the Weasel."

Reference

Alper, J. "Crazy Candies," *Chem Matters,* October 1993, 13.

Contributors

Paul Briese, Sand Ridge School, Lebanon, OR; Teaching Science with TOYS, 1994.
Barbie Dehm, Sand Ridge School, Lebanon, OR; Teaching Science with TOYS, 1994.
Jean McCormack, Liberty Elementary School, Liberty, IN; Teaching Science with TOYS, 1991–92.

Handout Master

A master for the following handout is provided:
- Pop Rocks Challenge—Observation Sheet
Copy as needed for classroom use.

Name _____   Date _____

Food that Pops
Pop Rocks Challenge—Observation Sheet

1 Describe the Pop Rocks before anything is done to them.	Sound	
	Feel	
	Other	
2 Describe the Pop Rocks you dropped water on.	Sound	
	Feel	
	Other	
3 Describe the Pop Rocks you put in your mouth.	Sound	
	Feel	
	Other	
4 Describe the Pop Rocks you held tightly in your hand.	Sound	
	Feel	
	Other	

combining the senses

5

I Can Sense You Like Popcorn

A Jar Full of Mystery

Mystery Boxes

I Can Sense You Like Popcorn

Students use their senses to investigate and enjoy popcorn.

Time Required

Setup	5 minutes
Performance	15–25 minutes
Cleanup	5 minutes

National Science Education Standards

Science as Inquiry Standards:

*   Abilities Necessary to Do Scientific Inquiry

    Students conduct a simple investigation in which they use all their senses to observe oil-popped and hot-air-popped popcorn and make systematic observations of each.

Physical Science Standards:

*   Properties of Objects and Materials

    The three states of matter are liquids, solids, and gases. This activity involves these states of matter and changes between them. Corn contains liquid water and starch within a solid kernel wall. Heat causes the liquid water to change state and become a gas (steam), thus exploding the kernel.

*   Light, Heat, Electricity, and Magnetism

    Heat is produced in the oil popper and the hot-air popper. The heat moves from the source to the kernel by conduction.

Popcorn—a feast for the senses

Materials

For the Procedure

Per class
*   unpopped popcorn
*   hot-air and hot-oil popcorn poppers
*   oil
*   oven mitt or potholder
*   2 large bowls
*   measuring cups
*   chart paper
*   markers

Per student
*   paper or plastic dish
*   napkin or paper towel

For Variations and Extensions

❶ Per class
- popcorn
- saucepan
- hot plate
- water

❷ All materials listed for the Procedure plus the following:
- various brands of popcorn

❸ Per class
- popcorn
- hot-air popcorn popper
- large bowl
- microwave-safe container
- access to a microwave

❹ All materials listed for the Procedure plus the following:
- cheese
- caramel
- spices
- butter or margarine

Safety and Disposal

Warn students not to touch the hot popcorn popper. Use an oven mitt or potholder when cooking. Birds and squirrels will enjoy leftover popcorn. This provides an important lesson on reducing unnecessary waste.

Introducing the Activity

Options:

- Ask students what they already know and what they want to know about popcorn. Record their responses on the board for later reference.

- Read *The Popcorn Book,* by Tomie de Paola. (See Cross-Curricular Integration.)

Procedure

1. Have the students look at popcorn kernels, feel them, and smell them.

2. Make popcorn using a hot-air popper and a hot-oil popper. Ask students, "As the popcorn heats, what senses tell you that a change is occurring?" *Smell, hearing, sight.*

3. Do not salt or butter the popped corn. Collect each of the two types of popcorn in a separate container. Label each for yourself but keep the identity from the students.

4. Give each student some of each kind of popcorn. Have the students compare the popcorn with unpopped kernels. Ask, "Do they look, smell, or feel the same?"

5. Allow the students to eat the popcorn. Remind them that they are using another sense—taste.

6. Ask them to identify which corn they think was popped in the hot-air popper and which in the hot-oil popper and to give evidence for the decision. (Popped corn made with hot oil often retains some oil, which is detectable by taste, touch, and sometimes smell.)

Variation and Extensions

1. Try popping kernels in hot water. (The corn does not pop because the water does not reach a high enough temperature before it boils, and enough steam cannot build up inside the kernel.)

2. Try various brands of popcorn in order to test for taste and amount popped. Graph results and chart words describing the brands' tastes.

3. Try popping equal amounts of one brand of popcorn in a popper and in a microwave. Determine which method popped the most kernels.

4. Make various types of popcorn—cheese, caramel, spiced, and buttered. Challenge students to identify the different varieties.

Explanation

 The following explanation is intended for the teacher's information. Modify the explanation for students as required.

Corn kernels are seeds with tough outer coats. Inside the coats, the kernels contain the plant embryo and stored food. The food is made of starch and water. Heat from the popper warms the kernels, causing the starch-water mixture to form a molten liquid. Some of the liquid water is converted into steam until over 8 atmospheres of pressure builds up. Steam, being a gas, occupies much more space than the same mass of liquid water. As the volume expands, the pressure created by this steam formation pushes harder against the inside of the kernel walls until the kernels explode. In the explosion, the steam is released so violently that it carries some of the liquid starch with it. The liquid starch quickly solidifies as it is cooled into the solid foam we know as popped corn.

Assessment

Have students write journal entries about what they learned about popcorn.

Cross-Curricular Integration

Language arts:

- Write a class activity story beginning with, "I am a popcorn kernel." Give each student an opportunity to contribute a sentence to the story. Emphasize that the story can be imaginary but should still use observations the students made during the activity.
- Read aloud or suggest that students read one or more of the following books:
  - *Cornzapoppin'!,* by Barbara Williams (Holt, Rinehart, and Winston, ISBN 0-030-1436-67)
    Popcorn recipes and party ideas for all occasions. A guide to the history, growing, buying, storing, popping, and flavoring of popcorn accompanies special recipes, decorating, and party ideas for occasions throughout the year.
  - *Popcorn,* by Millicent Selsam (Morrow, ISBN 0-688-2208-35)
    Describes the growth cycle of the type of corn used to make popcorn.
  - *The Popcorn Book,* by Tomie de Paola (Holiday House, ISBN 0-8234-0533-8)
    Presents a variety of facts about popcorn and includes two recipes.
  - *The Popcorn Dragon,* by Jane Thayer (Scholastic, ISBN 0-590-43609-0)
    Though his hot breath is the envy of all the other animals, a young dragon learns that showing off does not make friends.

Life science:

- Study the development of domesticated corn from its wild ancestor.
- Study the anatomy of a corn kernel.
- String the popcorn and hang it on trees and bushes for the birds during the winter.
- Discuss safety procedures for working around hot appliances and for cleanliness (for example, washing hands before eating).

Math:

- Have students compare the weight and volume of unpopped and popped corn.

Physical education:

- Have students act out a popcorn kernel popping.

Social studies:

- Have students investigate the history of popcorn.

Contributors

Michael Tominello, Donora Elementary Center, Donora, PA; Teaching Science with TOYS, 1994.
Ann Veith, Rosedale Elementary School, Middletown, OH; Teaching Science with TOYS, 1991–92.
John Wolf, Dixie Bee Elementary School, Terre Haute, IN; Teaching Science with TOYS, 1994.

A Jar Full of Mystery

Students observe the properties of solids and liquids while making butter.

Butter-making materials and the finished product

Time Required

Setup	10–15 minutes
Performance	20–25 minutes
Cleanup	10 minutes

National Science Education Standards

Science as Inquiry Standards:

- Abilities Necessary to Do Scientific Inquiry

  Students conduct a simple investigation in which they examine two liquids (whipping cream and skim milk) and a solid (butter) and make systematic observations using several of their senses.

Physical Science Standards:

- Properties of Objects and Materials

  The three states of matter are liquid, solid, and gas. This activity involves these states of matter and chemical reactions involving them. Students observe that a yellow solid (butter) can be produced from a white liquid (whipping cream) as a result of a chemical change.

Materials

For Getting Ready
Per class of 30 students
- 1 pint whipping cream (about 500 milliliters)
- about ½ cup 2% or skim milk (120 milliliters)
- 2 small dropper bottles or 2 large droppers
- masking tape and permanent marker or crayon for labels

Per group
- small, clear jar at least 100 milliliters (mL) in volume with tight-fitting lid

> *Clean the jars thoroughly before using them for this activity.*

For the Procedure
Per class
- 2 labeled dropper bottles or droppers of unknowns prepared in Getting Ready

189

Per group
- small jar with cream prepared in Getting Ready
- 2 paper cupcake cups
- toothpick
- plastic table knife

Per student
- napkin
- salted soda cracker

Safety and Disposal

Remind students never to taste an unknown substance unless permission is given by an adult in charge. No special disposal procedures are required.

Getting Ready

Pour 30–50 mL whipping cream into each jar. (Be sure the jars are not more than ¼ filled with cream.) Put the lids firmly on the jars. The cream should be room temperature when doing the activity.

Half-fill one small dropper bottle with cream and label it "A." Half-fill another dropper with 2% or skim milk and label it "B." These are your unknown white liquids. Label each group's cupcake cups "A" and "B."

Procedure

1. Put about five drops of liquid "A" into cupcake cup A and about five drops of "B" into cup B for each group.

2. Have the groups use toothpicks to move the drops around. Ask students to compare "A" and "B" liquids. How are they alike? *Both are white liquids.* Different? *A is thicker and more white than B.*

3. Pass out the jars containing the cream and ask students to examine them. Do not tell students that they are going to make butter. Tell students that the jars contain one of the unknown liquids. Without opening the jars, ask students to compare the behavior of the liquids in the cupcake cups and to identify which of the two liquids is in their jars.

4. Tell students the liquid in the jars reacts with oxygen in the air to form an interesting substance. Ask students to suggest how they might change the liquid to a solid. Have students in the groups take turns shaking the jars and observe what happens.

 Five minutes or more are required before the change from cream to butter takes place. Best results are obtained if shaking is continuous and vigorous.

5. When the jar feels like it has a ball inside, have students open the lid and observe the contents.

6. Explain that you can get a yellow solid from a white liquid because a chemical reaction occurred. Ask, "How does the color of the remaining liquid compare with the original?" *It is very watery-looking and only slightly white, much like the skim milk.*

7. Pass out plastic knives and salted crackers. Have students spread a little of the solid onto the crackers and taste it. Ask them to speculate what the solid may be.

 Stress the importance of never placing materials in the mouth or tasting things during science activities unless specifically directed by the teacher to do so.

Variations and Extensions

1. Carry out the activity using cold whipping cream. Compare the length of time it takes for the solid to form from cold whipping cream as opposed to the room-temperature whipping cream used in the Procedure.

2. Is it necessary to have air in the jar when making butter? Repeat the experiment with the jar full to the brim with cream and find out. *Yes, air is necessary; the experiment will not work if the jar is full to the brim.*

3. Have students do the "Homemade Butter" Take-Home Activity (provided) outside of school with an adult partner.

Explanation

 The following explanation is intended for the teacher's information. Modify the explanation for students as required.

In the initial part of the experiment, students compared whipping cream, which is 30–36% milk fat, to skim or 2% milk, which is 0.1–2% milk fat. The different amounts of milk fat give these liquids their different properties. The three liquids are, however, similar in that the milk fat is suspended as very small droplets in a watery liquid. Because these droplets are so small, they remain suspended evenly throughout the liquid and make the liquid appear to be homogeneous. Mixtures of this type that consist of small droplets of liquids suspended in a liquid are called emulsions.

The shaking of the whipping cream allows the droplets of milk fat to react with the oxygen from the air trapped in the jar. In the process, the small droplets coalesce into large clumps of butter which float to the surface of the liquid. The color change is an indication that a chemical reaction occurred. This reaction with oxygen is called an air oxidation reaction. While a similar oxidation reaction could occur with the 2% or skim milk, the amount of milk fat present is too low in these liquids to yield the same results.

Assessment

Have students complete the "How to Make Butter" Assessment Sheet (provided).

Cross-Curricular Integration

Home, safety, and career:
- Have students bring in various butter and margarine packages. Compare calories and fat content. Point out that all fats have the same number of calories per gram. You may wish to have students compare the taste, texture, and color of margarine, homemade butter, and purchased butter.

Language arts:
- Have students interview a grandparent or elderly neighbor and see if this person ever made butter. Have students write narrative paragraphs of their interviews.
- Read aloud or suggest that students read one or more of the following books:
  ○ *From Grass to Butter,* by Ali Mitgutsch (Carolrhoda, ISBN 0-87614-156-4)
     Briefly explains how grass is used by cows to produce milk which can be made into butter.
  ○ *Milk from Cow to Carton,* by Aliki (HarperTrophy, ISBN 0-06-445111-9)
     Briefly describes how a cow produces milk, how the milk is processed in a dairy, and how various other dairy products are made from milk.
  ○ *Pancakes for Breakfast,* by Tomie dePaola (Scholastic, ISBN 0-590-45136-7)
     A woman goes through many mishaps and much work (including churning butter) before she can finally have the pancakes for breakfast that she has been longing for.

Social studies:
- Have students research how butter was made and stored during the pioneer days and how it is made, shipped, and stored today.

Reference

Jones, E.; Jones, S. "A Jarful of Mystery," *Science and Children.* 1983, 20(4), 18–19.

Sarquis, M.; Kibbey, B.; Smyth, E. "A Jar Full of Mystery," *Science Activities for Elementary Classrooms;* Flinn Scientific: Batavia, IL, 1989; pp 1–4.

Contributors

Rosemary Klare, Ramey School, Ramey, PR; Teaching Science with TOYS, 1994.

Bob Roszell, Charles T. Young Elementary School, Cleves, OH; Teaching Science with TOYS, 1994.

Tomma Rychener, Charles T. Young Elementary School, Cleves, OH; Teaching Science with TOYS, 1994.

Nola Wilkinson, Johns Hill Magnet School, Decatur, IL; Teaching Science with TOYS, 1994.

Handout Masters

Masters for the following handouts are provided:
- Homemade Butter—Take-Home Activity
- How to Make Butter—Assessment Sheet

Copy as needed for classroom use.

A Jar Full of Mystery
Homemade Butter—Take-Home Activity

Date   _____

Dear Adult Partner(s):

Today in class we made butter from whipping cream by putting the cream in jars and shaking it. We tasted our butter and talked about the chemistry of milk and butter. In the initial part of the experiment, students compared whipping cream, which is 30–36% milk fat, to skim or 2% milk, which is 0.1–2% milk fat. The amount of milk fat gives these liquids different properties. The three liquids are, however, similar in that the milk fat is suspended as very small droplets in a watery liquid. Because these droplets are so small, they remain suspended evenly throughout the liquid and make the liquid appear to be homogeneous.

Shaking or churning whipping cream allows the droplets of milk fat to react with oxygen from the air trapped in the jar. In the process, the small droplets coalesce into large clumps of butter which float to the surface of the water. The color change is an indication that a chemical reaction occurred. This reaction with oxygen is called an air oxidation reaction. While a similar oxidation reaction could occur with 2% or skim milk, the amount of milk fat present is too low in these liquids to yield the same results.

Attached is an alternative procedure that uses a homemade butter churn. Please help your child make the churn and try out this preparation. Enjoy your butter-making experiment!

Sincerely,

_____

A Jar Full of Mystery

Homemade Butter—Take-Home Activity, page 2

Materials

- 1-pint margarine tub with lid
- drinking straw (the bigger the better)
- scissors
- ½ pint whipping cream
- salt
- bread or salted crackers

Fold the flaps so they are 90° from the rest of the straw.

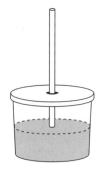

Put the dasher in the tub with the handle sticking through the tub lid.

Making the Churn

1. Cut the bottom 1½ inches of the straw into fourths. Fold these segments so they radiate out from the center of the straw at 90° angles. This apparatus is called the dasher.

2. Cut a hole in the tub lid wide enough for the handle of the dasher to fit through.

3. Pour the cream into the margarine tub.

4. Put the dasher in the tub and fasten the lid so that the handle of the dasher sticks up through the hole. You're ready to churn!

Churning the Butter

1. Move the dasher up and down very fast. After a while, the cream will turn into whipped cream. Continue churning, and lumps of butter will appear. The lumps will get bigger and bigger until they form one big lump. Pour off the leftover liquid (buttermilk).

2. Spread the unsalted butter on a salted cracker or mix salt into the butter to taste and spread it on a piece of bread. Enjoy!

Reproduced from *Exploring Matter with **TOYS***, published by McGraw-Hill.

Name _____   Date _____

A Jar Full of Mystery
How to Make Butter—Assessment Sheet

In this activity, we made butter from cream. Draw four pictures to show four steps in making and taste-testing butter.

Mystery Boxes

*Students realize the value of using their senses
(in this case, hearing, touch, and possibly smell) in combination.*

. . . .

Time Required

Setup   10 minutes
Performance   20 minutes
Cleanup   less than 5 minutes

National Science Education Standards

Mystery boxes and objects

Science as Inquiry Standards:

- Abilities Necessary to Do Scientific Inquiry

  Students use their own observations to answer the question "Which
  sample object matches the object in the mystery box?"

  Students conduct a simple investigation in which they use their
  senses of touch, hearing, and possibly smell to observe the sample
  items and the items in Mystery Boxes and make systematic
  observations of each.

  They formulate a hypothesis about what is in the box and appeal to
  the evidence they obtained to support their hypothesis.

Physical Science Standards:

- Properties of Objects and Materials

  The objects are made of one or more materials and can be described
  by the properties of the materials from which they are made. These
  properties can be used to match each mystery object's identity with
  a sample object.

. . . .

Materials

For Getting Ready
Per group
- duplicate pairs of several mystery objects, such as the following:
  ◦ wooden blocks of different sizes and shapes (for example, cylinder, sphere,
    rectangular prism, cone, cube)
  ◦ balls
  ◦ marbles
  ◦ corks
  ◦ bottle caps
  ◦ pens or pencils
  ◦ coins
- opaque box with a lid or flap that is easily opened and reclosed, such as a
  shoebox

197

For the Procedure

Per group

- Mystery Box prepared in Getting Ready
- 3 objects, 1 of which is identical to the object in the group's Mystery Box

For Variations and Extensions

❷ Per class

- large box
- 2 pieces of fabric
- pair of socks
- variety of objects

Safety and Disposal

No special safety or disposal procedures are required.

Getting Ready

Prepare a Mystery Box for each group by placing one object in a box with a lid. Be sure you have a duplicate of that object available for examination.

Introducing the Activity

Without revealing its identity, place an object in a box that the students are unable to see into. Ask the students to guess what may be in the box. Do not allow the object to move around or students to handle the box. After several guesses are offered, ask the students why they had so much difficulty guessing the object. *No clues were given about the object.* Ask the students what would help them make better guesses without opening the box. *Shake the box, feel the weight, etc.*

Procedure

1. Give each group a Mystery Box and instruct students to keep the box closed during the exploration steps of the activity.

2. Give each group three objects and explain that one of these objects is identical to the object in the group's Mystery Box.

3. Instruct the group to examine the box without opening or peeking into it. Allow each student in the group to spend several minutes examining the box.

4. Challenge each group to formulate a hypothesis about what is in its box and to provide evidence to support its idea.

5. Allow each group to open its box to reveal the actual identity of the mystery object.

6. Provide the students with pairs of identical objects and allow the groups to make their own Mystery Boxes and trade with other groups. Repeat Steps 3–5.

Variations and Extensions

1. Place two or three objects in a Mystery Box. Have the students try to describe and identify each item separately.

2. On opposite sides of a box, cut holes large enough for students to put hands and forearms in. Cut a piece of fabric to cover each hole and tape it inside the box at the top of the hole to form a flap. Place several objects in the box. Have a student put socks on his or her hands and slide the sock-covered hands through the holes in the sides of the box. Challenge the student to describe and guess the identity of each object in the box.

Explanation

The following explanation is intended for the teacher's information. Modify the explanation for students as required.

Scientists often confront situations in which they cannot directly see what they are investigating. Thus, they must use other experimental evidence to gather information. For example, chemists cannot see atoms, but they infer information about them through methods such as observing the results of chemical reactions. In this activity, students rely on their senses of hearing and touch to observe what happens when the box is tipped gently from one side to another, quickly tipped, slowly tipped, or inverted. They use the different sounds and feelings to gather information about their object which helps them match it with one of the known objects.

Cross-Curricular Integration

Language arts:
- Scientists need to be able to clearly describe results of investigations. An important part of description is effective use of adjectives. Have students make lists of adjectives to describe the objects from the Mystery Boxes. Discuss which sense is used to identify the characteristic each adjective describes. For example, if an object can be described with the adjective "bumpy," the senses of sight, touch, and hearing may have been used.

Contributors

Damian Dagenbach, Hopewell Elementary School, West Chester, OH; Teaching Science with TOYS, 1994.

Michael Lolli, Hopewell Elementary School, West Chester, OH; Teaching Science with TOYS, 1994.

Appendix

National Science Education Standards Matrix

National Science Education Standards Matrix

This matrix shows how the activities in this book relate to the National Science Education Standards. The standards are taken from *National Science Education Standards*; National Research Council; National Academy: Washington, D.C., 1996.

	Activities			
	Are All Mittens the Same?	Balloon in a Bottle	Big Ben	Corn Starch Putty
Science as Inquiry Standards				
Abilities Necessary to Do Scientific Inquiry				
Ask a question about objects, organisms, and events in the environment.	✔			
Plan and conduct a simple investigation.	✔		✔	✔
Employ simple equipment and tools to gather data and extend the senses.	✔			
Use data to construct a reasonable explanation.		✔		
Communicate investigations and explanations.				
Physical Science Standards				
Properties of Objects and Materials				
Objects have many observable properties, including size, weight, shape, color, temperature, and the ability to react with other substances. Those properties can be measured using tools, such as rulers, balances, and thermometers.	✔		✔	✔
Objects are made of one or more materials, such as paper, wood, and metal. Objects can be described by the properties of the materials from which they are made, and those properties can be used to separate or sort a group of objects or materials.				✔
Materials can exist in different states—solid, liquid, and gas. Some common materials, such as water, can be changed from one state to another by heating or cooling.		✔		
Position and Motion of Objects				
Sound is produced by vibrating objects. The pitch of the sound can be varied by changing the rate of vibration.			✔	
Light, Heat, Electricity, and Magnetism				
Heat can be produced in many ways, such as burning, rubbing, or mixing one substance with another. Heat can move from one object to another by conduction.	✔			

Activities

Feely Balloons	Fixed and Unfixed Shapes	Food that Pops	Gluep	I Can Sense You Like Popcorn	Identifying Substances by Smell	A Jar Full of Mystery	Jumbled-Up Jello	M&M Classification	Mystery Boxes	Paper Cup Telephone	The Scratch-and-Sniff Challenge	Smelly Balloons	Tissue in a Cup	Using Taste to Solve a Mystery
									✔					
✔	✔	✔	✔	✔	✔	✔	✔	✔	✔	✔	✔	✔		✔
✔							✔		✔				✔	✔
✔		✔	✔			✔					✔			✔
	✔	✔	✔	✔		✔					✔	✔		
	✔						✔	✔						✔
		✔	✔		✔						✔	✔		
										✔				
			✔											

Activities Indexed by Science Topics

About The Author

Terrific Science Press is a nonprofit publisher housed in the federally and state-funded Center for Chemical Education (Miami University Middletown in Ohio). At the Center, educators and scientists have worked together since the mid-1980's to provide professional development for teachers through innovative approaches to teaching hands-on, minds-on science.